MY WORD!

for Bill Lopez
with the very best wishes
of the author —

Vivian Laughlin jr

Canyon Lake CA
Feb 90

MY WORD!

Celebrities Reveal their Favorite Words

&

the Reasons Behind their Selections

Compiled and Edited

By

Vick Knight, Jr., Ed.D.

With a Foreword by Richard Armour

Aristan Press

Aristan Press
31566 Railroad Canyon Road #612
Canyon Lake, CA 92587

First Edition
Copyright ©1996 by Vick Knight, Jr., Ed.D.

Cover design by Linda Germar Hoffman.

All rights reserved. Except for brief quotations in critical reviews or articles, no part of this publication may be reproduced, stored in a retrieval system or transmitted in any form or by any means, electronic, mechanical, photocopying, recording or otherwise without the written permission of the publisher.

Library of Congress Catalog Card Number 95-083087
ISBN 0-931407-03-6

Printed in the United States of America

For my mama
who, when I had only one word,
was it.

Introduction

The Gospel according to John tells us, "In the beginning was the Word."
Words have continued to perform a major function in virtually every event since primitive people first learned to give meanings to specific sounds. As an amateur semanticist and one who revels in a challenging crossword puzzle as well as a no-words-barred Scrabble game, I've discovered a few favorite words over the years. Some have intrigued me as a result of their enchanting derivations; others have intonations and cadences I have found especially pleasing to my ears. There are certain words I associate with a memorable usage; others are fun to use judiciously in light of their being somewhat esoteric or eccentric. I've rarely been accused of eschewing obfuscation.

Some years ago, the thought occurred to me that it might prove rewarding to learn if others were willing to select a single word from the dictionary's vast collection as their very own and then reveal to me the rationale for its selection.

As many today tend to depend more and more on counterfeit words of their own dubious coinage and, in almost epidemic proportions, to lace their conversation with weak portmanteau words and sparring intercalations such as the ubiquitous "y'know," "well" and "okay?", educators are increasingly aware of the need for strengthening the average vocabulary. It's my conviction that a new and vigorous interest in words can be generated if we present them in conjunction with distinctive applications and fortify these choices with authoritative sponsorship such as those who have contributed to this volume.

This book contains a sampling from the several hundred responses I received from the following request :
May I have a word with you?
More precisely, may I have a word from you?

More than fifty percent of those solicited took the time to answer my letter. Some responses were single words scrawled across my original request and returned to me. Others involved thoughtful and lengthy descriptions of the reason behind the selection.

Among the first to reply with a favorite word was Dr. Richard Armour. It's been suggested that he wore two costumes: cap-and-gown and cap-and-bells. Dr. Armour held a Harvard Ph.D. in philology, which explains his love for words. He wrote several scholarly biographies, taught at a number of colleges and universities, lectured or was writer-in-residence on more than three hundred campuses, and addressed groups in both Asia and Europe on behalf of the State Department.

As for the cap-and-bells, he wrote close to sixty books on humor and satire, in prose and in light verse, and contributed more than six thousand articles and poems to leading magazines in the United States and England. He was not only prolific but also a perfectionist, always trying to put the right word in the right place. I was honored when he graciously accepted my invitation to expand his original contribution to serve as the Foreword to this book . We liked the idea of a title page that reads "MY WORD! by Knight with Armour."

Among the more succinct replies was one from the celebrated NFL coach George Allen. His simple comment, "My favorite word is win!" adequately sums up his philosophy, his lifestyle, and the accomplishments of his football teams. T (which stands for nothing) George Harris, one time editor-in-chief of the publication *Psychology Today*, tersely commented: "My word for the day is hogwash. Perhaps you will supply the apologia if any be needed."

I decided that no defense was necessary for that word or for the one superimposed upon my letter by publisher Ralph Ginzburg, capitalized and complete with exclamation point: "BALDERDASH!"

A surprising number of respondents indicated no special preference for a specific word, yet took the time to encourage me in my quest. Eighty-two year-old chewing gum magnate Philip K. Wrigley wrote: "I have no favorite word or words that I could write about. In fact, I try to use as few words as possible as it is the best protection I have been able to find not to be misquoted."

Amy Vanderbilt displayed her consummate manners in courteously declining my invitation to participate. Isaac Asimov, author of the astounding total of more than three hundred books on a universal range of subjects from the dynamics of asteroids to the intricacies of Shakespeare, refused in this manner:

"I thought about it and I really don't have a favorite word and even if I make one up, it will mean getting a picture to you, and making up some soppy paragraph or other, and—well, I just don't want to."

As a result of the above, I've already managed to slip "soppy" into several conversations where, in the past, I had to make do with "mawkish."

Sister Corita Kent, whose polychromatic serigraphs I've collected and cherished, simply said: "Sorry, no. Writing is too much."

Potential correspondents were selected from contemporary personalities on the basis of two criteria: those solicited were persons whose responses would reasonably be expected to be authoritative and would represent the opinions of renowned individuals. The ultimate utilization of specific answers was a function of the editor's prerogative.

Author Walter Lord indicated that he tries to avoid being a slave to a favorite word. He remarked, "When I find myself using a word too much, I try to veer away from it for a while. Like a good baseball pitcher, a good writer should vary his delivery."

Ira (*Rosemary's Baby*) Levin replied via postcard as follows: "Sorry, but I'm in the middle of a play and need every word I've got."

While it's true I didn't hear directly from J. Paul Getty, his secretary, Miss Carole M. Tier, wrote from Sutton Place, Surrey, England, that the word he'd chosen was "fact," and she sent me the following quote:

"It is important to distinguish a fact. A fact must be a fact, and an opinion must be recognised as only an opinion. Many people state an opinion as through it were a fact." It's my considered opinion that Mr. Getty's impressive wealth may have had something to do with his propensity for dealing in facts.

Basketball Hall of Fame member and Los Angeles Laker executive Bill Sharman's response was short and sweet: "When the going gets tough, the tough get going!"

Washington Post columnist and Pulitzer Prize winner Mary McGrory chose two words: "My favorite words are 'summer afternoon.' They are beautiful in themselves, and they conjure up memories of sunny hours by my favorite lake in Antrim, New Hampshire, or by Robert Kennedy's swimming pool filled with happy poor children whom Ethel Kennedy let us bring every Thursday afternoon."

Of all the welcome responses I received, only one bore a caveat. This was the warning with which Dr. Edward Teller began his reply:

"The following paragraph, which I put in quotes, may be included in your book, if you wish, provided it is done without any alteration."

If the reader thinks I plan to mess with the father of the hydrogen bomb, think again. Here's the quote: "My two favorite words are megabuck and microdamn. The first is what you need (often several times over) to carry out respectable practical research. The second is what you do not give, provided you really do not care."

And, hotel executive Conrad N. Hilton wrote: "If I could choose but one word of the English language, that word would be faith. To me, the power implied in this word is almost inconceivable. It is the bond between man and his maker, the strongest tie that can exist between members of the human race, and the only basis for understanding and peaceful existence between nations of the world."

Amen.

Vick Knight, Jr.
Canyon Lake, California
1996

Foreword

by

Richard Armour

As the word "foreword" indicates, it is the word or words in the fore, ahead of the other words in a book. Always the foreword should look forward to what follows, just as the backword, if this book contained one, would look backward. The writer of the foreword has a special responsibility when the book is one about words.

It helps to know the book has been assembled by Vick Knight, who is always up to something, whether a practical joke, a serious book, or service for some humanitarian cause. Whatever he does he does well and with enthusiasm. It has been four years since he told me about his plans for this book and asked me to write the foreword. I do not know how many years he had already been corresponding, collecting, and assembling materials. It was not an easy task, although "task" is far from his favorite word, in fact not in his everyday vocabulary.

I am sure Vick enjoyed bringing this book into being. There were no labor pains. What he would now enjoy is having readers enjoy it, learn from it, even be inspired by it.

What struck me first when I read the manuscript, was the wide variety of busy people who answered Vick's query and sent him their favorite word and told him why it was their favorite. As you will see, they range from

Lucille Ball to Edward Teller, from Herman Wouk to Pat Nixon, from Erma Bombeck to Admiral Elmo Zumwalt, from Ann Landers to Joan Crawford, and from Lawrence Welk to Dr. Joyce Brothers.

There are scientists, political figures, high-ranking military men, preachers of various denominations, columnists, composers, novelists, sportsmen, cartoonists, personalities of stage and screen, and well-known men and women in just about every field. Among them is an ingenious player with words, Willard Espy, and a scholarly linguist, Mario Pei.

Once I had been impressed by the variety and quality of contributors, I was fascinated by the favorite word each had chosen. You can tell a man by the company he keeps (or the company he owns). You can tell a woman by the company she invites. And you can tell something about a man or woman by that person's choice of a favorite word.

Here again there is a great range, all the way from "yes" to "no." Interestingly, very few persons chose the same word. Some like a word for its sound, some for its significance in human relations, some for an incident in their life. There is a difference in mood between the choice of "crisis" or "inevitable" and that of "beauty" or "caring" or "freedom." But I must not give away all the words you will soon discover for yourself, or link the word to the person. The latter is what gives the book an element of surprise and will keep you moving from one person and word to another.

One reason I liked this book is because I am a word man. I call the room in which I write not my workshop but my wordshop, and I sometimes envy Wordsworth, who had the ideal name for a writer. The dictionary is my favorite book, the book I take to bed with me when I am sick and the book I would choose to have with me if I were marooned on a desert island. While I am at the typewriter, I am surrounded by dictionaries: old, new, big, little, American, British, and those that help with foreign languages.

Sometimes I play a little game, flipping the pages of a dictionary back and forth and invariably discovering a word that interests me. Such a word is "slubberdegullion," which is defined as "a mean wretch, a base, slovenly boor." When I ran across this, I could hardly wait to use it on the first slubberdegullion I met. I felt safe, should he be bigger than I, because I would have time to flee while he was getting to a dictionary to look up the word.

Coleridge made a succinct differentiation between prose and poetry, based on words. "Prose," he said, "is words in their best order; poetry is the best words in their best order."

Words, to me, are not only long and short, but light and heavy, rough and smooth. I fit words together as a stonemason fits stones. They are not only essential to me in expressing myself, they often give me an idea and start me writing. Indeed, I owe so much to words and am such a lover of words that I suppose my own favorite word is "word."

But you will find more interesting words, and more surprising connections between favorite words and those who chose them, in the pages that follow. This is only a foreword, or foretaste, of what is to come.

Table of Contents

Introduction	vii
Foreword	xi
Willard Scott	1
President Ronald Reagan	2
Dick DeVos	4
Ronald McDonald	6
Willard Espy	7
Dr. Leo Buscaglia	8
Ronnie Milsap	10
Erma Bombeck	12
Abigail Van Buren	14
Dr. Robert Schuller	16
Nick Meglin	18
Frank Deford	20
Patricia Nixon	22
Carl Karcher	24
Stephen King	26
Herbert D. Eagle	27
Dr. Bernie Siegel	28
Danny Cox	30
Mary Kay Ash	33
Lawrence Welk	34
General Robinson Risner	36
Tom Landry	38
Dr. Paul Popenoe	39
Admiral Elmo Zumwalt	40
Father Theodore Hesburgh	42
Meredith Willson	43
Jimmy Dean	44
Robert Mondavi	46
Letitia Baldridge	48
Michael Crichton	50

Jack Kemp	52
Dave Barry	54
Kate White	56
Mary Renault	57
Father Malcolm Boyd	58
Chuck Jonak	60
Tom Harmon	62
Stephen Ambrose	64
Fletcher Knebel	66
Dr. David Viscott	68
Timothy Forbes	70
Roger Staubach	72
Lee Hills	73
Ralph deToledano	74
Bart Starr	76
Santa Claus	78
Milton Caniff	80
Walter Knott	82
Vin Scully	84
George Gallup, Jr.	86
Harry Golden	87
Joan Dial	88
Ann Landers	90
Mario Pei	91
Lucille Ball	92
Pat Boone	94
Rev. Billy Graham	96
Joan Embery	99
William Anders	100
David Wolper	101
Herman Wouk	102
Glen Campbell	104
Christine Todd Whitman	106

Colonel Harland Sanders 108
Dr. Joyce Brothers 110
Lowell Thomas 113
President Gerald Ford 114
Larry Speakes 116
Walter Brennan 118
Dan Jansen 121
Joan Crawford 122
Robert Bloch 123
Fran Capo 124
Nancy Kassebaum 126
L. Ron Hubbard 128
Cesar Romero 131
Barry Goldwater 132
Dr. Morris Fishbein 133
Dr. Giles Brown 134
Eugene McCarthy 137
Bob Mathias 138
Art Linkletter 140
Michael Strumpf 142
Johnny Mercer 144
Hank Ketcham 146
Index by Name 149
Index by Word 152

Willard Scott

The ebullient Willard Scott has made mornings much brighter for millions of viewers since he first appeared on "Today" in 1980 reporting the nation's weather. In addition to his many weather telecasts from state fairs, fund-raising events, parades and civic affairs, he has traveled with "Today" throughout Europe, aboard the Orient Express, to China and Australia, to Rome during Holy Week and to the heartland of America.

The author of four books, Scott is a graduate of American University in Washington, D.C., with a degree in Philosophy and Religion. He is a native of Virginia and was recognized by President Ronald Reagan with the Private Sector Award for Public Service.

God

I have been very fortunate. From my earliest childhood the awareness of God's presence in my life was always taught to me.

God has blessed me with much happiness and success. God sustained me during my failures. God consoled me in my grief. God walks with me during my life, and when I cannot go any farther, God will carry me.

President Ronald Reagan

Ronald Wilson Reagan was the fortieth President of the United States. Born in Tampico, Illinois, in 1911, he graduated from Eureka College and worked as a sportscaster for several radio stations in the Midwest. Discovered by a Hollywood agent, he joined Warner Brothers, making his debut in Love is On the Air *(1937). He appeared in a total of fifty-two feature movies, with memorable roles in* Brother Rat *(1938),* Dark Victory *(1939) and* Kings Row *(1941). He made training films for the Air Force in World War II and served as a spokesman for the General Electric Company, hosting and occasionally acting on the television series "General Electric Theater." Shifting from the Democratic Party, he moved into Republican politics and, with the 1964 presidential election, emerged as a Goldwater Conservative. In 1966 he was elected governor of California. He was the Republican candidate for President in 1980 and beat Jimmy Carter in that race. Four years later he defeated Walter Mondale by a landslide. He was in office for eight years.*

MY WORD!

Home

In trying to decide on my favorite word, I selected and then discarded several. Only one word seems always to have had special meaning and importance to me. That word is **home**.

As far back as I can remember, home has brought an immediate mental image and almost tangible feeling of comfort, happiness and well-being. Home is synonymous with love and acceptance and being totally at ease. As a boy, home meant someone waiting, a place to immodestly enjoy success and openly suffer failure and a place to regain a perspective on important and seemingly important achievements and discoveries.

Now as an adult, home still has all those same meanings and, in addition, is a place where I know as I approach the door, someone is waiting for the sound of my footsteps. I count that fact among my greatest blessings.

Dick DeVos

President of the worldwide marketing phenomenon Amway Corporation, Dick DeVos is following in the footsteps of his father, Amway founder Richard DeVos, as head of this billion-dollar international direct sales distribution network. He began working for Amway in 1974, and in 1984, was named vice president - International, responsible for the operation of Amway's affiliate companies in eighteen countries. Under his leadership, sales more than tripled, and international sales exceeded domestic sales for the first time in the company's history.

In 1989, the entrepreneurial heritage of his family took him into his own business. He founded The Windquest Group, focusing attention on storage and space utilization products. In 1991, following the family's acquisition of the Orlando Magic professional basketball team, Dick became the president and CEO of the NBA franchise. Two years later, he was asked to return to Amway and take up the company's reins as its president, succeeding his father.

He continues to serve on numerous public, professional and civic boards including the Michigan State Board of Education, the White House Commission on Presidential Scholars, National Association of Manufacturers, and the West Michigan Boy Scouts.

Hope

As president of a business that gives anyone the opportunity to realize a dream through effort and determination, a key word for me is **hope**.

Our free enterprise system and the American dream are only possible because of the hope for things yet to be seen. Our country was discovered and settled by people of hope. Our nation's two centuries of progress, our many advances in science and technology, our economic growth, our faith that each of us is part of God's plan with God-given talents that we can fulfill to their potential, and our belief that we can provide something better for our children can all be summed up in that simple word, hope. Around the world, people are striving to improve themselves, their communities and their societies because within the human spirit is the hope that life can always be better.

Hope is highest when the need is greatest. All is not lost if we do not lose hope. Hope is our heart telling us to keep going when our head tells us to turn back. Hope turns darkness into dawn — easing our fears, erasing our doubts, and making us believe anything is possible. I have seen the power of hope carry people from poverty to wealth and from despair to joy. Hope is a wonderful thing, and ultimately, Isaiah said it well in his fortieth chapter: *But those who hope in the Lord will renew their strength. They will soar on wings like eagles. They will run and not grow weary. They will walk and not be faint.*

Ronald McDonald

Ronald McDonald made his first public appearance in Washington, D.C., in 1963 and made his first national television appearance in the Macy's Thanksgiving Day Parade in 1966. In 1969 he became McDonald's worldwide spokesperson and now speaks more than twenty-one languages.

Ronald is loved by children around the world because he's more than a clown. He's magical. He's funny. He's smart. He's friendly. He's caring. He's a leader. Most of all, he's the best friend a kid could imagine, and he always loves to make them laugh.

Laughter

Laughter is my favorite word. I always share a laugh or a grin with people I know and those I don't know because it always seems to brighten everyone's day. And I always tell kids to keep an extra smile in their pocket to share with people they meet.

Laughter is great, too, because it defies gravity. It's good for you, and everybody loves to do it. It's an all-purpose pick-me-up that anyone can use, anytime and anywhere!

MY WORD!

Willard Espy

After a period with the Readers' Digest, *Willard Espy wrote, produced and served as the interviewer on a radio series called "Personalities of the Past." His books include* The Game of Words, Say It My Way, The Garden of Eloquence, Words to Rhyme With *and* An Almanac of Words at Play. *He accompanied his serious endeavors with a delight in the frivolity of language. His light verse and critical articles appeared in numerous publications.*

Behemoth

If I were Diogenes' honest man, the word I would submit would be "I." It is by all odds my favorite. I put it to use at every opportunity, and if it does not appear often enough in a sentence like this one, I go back and I write that sentence over.

The difficulty is that if the rest of the contributors to this book were as honest as I, they would submit the same word—and you can't very well have a vocabulary builder with nothing but "I" in it, can you? So I shall settle for **behemoth.** Now there's a word! Victor Proetz said it was drawn "at the same overwhelming scale as Michelangelo's ceiling." And you can have the luxury of pronouncing it correctly in three different ways, as I do here:

Behold Now Behemoth!
Behold now where by Jordan dreameth
The handiwork of God, Be - he' - moth.
Author He of Man, but Auth-
or no less of Be' - he - moth.
Praise to Him Who made us both,
Homo sap. and Be - he - moth —
Man and beast, like Him, trichotomous.
(Too bad it just means Hip-po-pot'-a-mus.)

Dr. Leo Buscaglia

Educator, author and lecturer Leo Buscaglia has a Ph.D. from the University of Southern California and is dedicated to encouraging and teaching the spirit of giving in our society. His first book, Love, *was originally published in 1972 and has never been out of print. More than eleven million copies of his books have been sold, and* Love, Loving and Learning, *and* Loving Each Other *have each sold over a million copies.*

Editions of Dr. Buscaglia's books are available in nineteen languages. The Fall of Freddie the Leaf *has been adapted in audio cassette, educational film and a one-hour ballet, and* A Memory for Tino, *his only book specifically for children, has been adapted to video for distribution to schools throughout the United States.*

A contributing editor to Positive Living *magazine, Dr. Buscaglia was one of the first ten inductees in the Hershey's Hugs Hall of Fame.*

Love

As you can imagine, my favorite word is **love**.

Not only because it has been a faithful companion to me for over seventy years of life and because I have spent over half of that lifetime attempting to understand and study it, but also because I have been in constant awe as to the power and magic it continually creates when verbalized and acted upon.

Still, love remains the most desecrated of all words, as we batter it about to suit our own purposes.

The term knows no definition. In fact, to define it would be to delimit it. Love grows as we grow and changes as we change. It would be safe to say that it becomes deeper, more profound and dynamic with each loving day of our lives.

Who cannot be in love with love?

Ronnie Milsap

Ronnie Milsap

Born blind in the shadow of the Great Smoky Mountains, Ronnie Milsap found the light of music in the special school he attended in North Carolina. He became proficient on violin, cello, clarinet, guitar, piano and vocals and scored his first hit with "Never Had It So Good." By 1976, he was touring the world's great concert halls while headlining his own show.

In 1982, his recording of "Any Day Now" was chosen by Billboard *as Song of the Year, and in 1983, "Stranger in My House" was the Grammy Award-winning single. Milsap has been named the Country Music Association's Entertainer of the Year and Male Vocalist of the Year, and is the recipient of the only gold braille album ever awarded. His autobiography,* Almost Like a Song, *was published by McGraw-Hill.*

MY WORD!

Challenge

If I had to give a summation of my life into one word, it would be **challenge**.

Words have power, and I like everything about this word.

It is strong. There can be no misinterpretation of it, whether it is used as a noun or a verb, it means motion, and I like that!

Challenge means you've tried something, whether or not you've succeeded or have been understood, you've tried something.

I seem to incorporate challenge into every phase of my music; always asking myself what I can give that is better or different, and I believe that is what keeps life fresh.

Erma Bombeck

Photo by Stephen Van Worner

Erma Bombeck is the best-selling author of such humorous books as The Grass Grows Greener Over the Septic Tank; At Wit's End; Just Wait Till You Have Children of Your Own; Motherhood: the Second Oldest Profession; If Life is a Bowl of Cherries, What Am I Doing in the Pits?; All I Know About Animal Behavior I Learned in Loehmann's Dressing Room *and* Aunt Erma's Cope Book. *Her columns are found in hundreds of newspapers from coast to coast, and she captures the interest of millions of fans with her droll commentaries on everyday events taking place in her family. She enjoys a position very close to the cat-bird seat of American humor as a consequence of the relationship she has developed with those who have come in contact with her wit and insight.*

In addition to her literary successes, she's been on the cover of TIME magazine and has the honor of being recognized consistently by the World Almanac *as one of the Twenty-Five Most Influential Women in America.*

MY WORD!

Yes

As a humorist, my favorite word has to be **yes**.

To begin with, I can spell it without going to my ten-pound hernia edition of Webster's dictionary.

Secondly, you cannot imagine the excitement the word yes exuberates.

I first discovered this when a program chairman asked, "Are you finished speaking?" When I said "yes," I got a standing ovation. I was so impressed, I started using it more and more. When my children asked, "May I go down the Mississippi River on a raft with Orville this summer?" and I'd say, "yes," they would turn to me and say, "You're the neatest mother ever."

Yes is happiness, agreement, consent and affirmation. I don't know where yes will lead me . . . so far I chair 24 committees, lead a troop of fat Girl Scouts, have the attention of 18 obscene phone callers, have 2 1/2 too many children, 35 magazine subscriptions and support 3 political parties.

And, when Vick Knight, Jr. wrote and say,
"May I have a word from you?" the answer was yea.

Abigail Van Buren

Though she was born Pauline Esther Friedman, Abigail Van Buren launched her advice column in 1956 as "Dear Abby." (She took her pen name from that of President Martin Van Buren's daughter-in-law, who was the White House hostess during his term in office.)

Her column is now internationally syndicated and appears daily in newspapers responding to letters from an adoring public. Her books include The Best of Dear Abby, Dear Abby on Planning Your Wedding and How to Have a Lovely Wedding.

Abigail Van Buren has been an active and vocal advocate for health reforms and has received many public service awards and citations. She is the twin sister of the journalist known as Ann Landers.

No

As much as I respect, admire and love Erma Bombeck, whose favorite word is yes—my favorite word is **no**!

When a person says no (emphatically), he/she is immediately relieved of assuming a responsibility he or she did not wish to be stuck with. Example: "Will you please assume the chairmanship of the Mothers' and Daughters' annual banquet again this year? You did such a great job of it <u>last</u> year—and the year before." Or, "Would you mind signing this petition to support Newt Gingrich in his plan to promote orphanages?"

After responding to a question with a firm, audible no, leave no time for a follow-up question. Simply say no and either change the subject or walk away.

It takes years to gather the gumption to say no—but the rewards are gratifying.

I could not, however, say no to your request for a favorite word!

Dr. Robert Schuller

Dr. Robert Schuller

Robert H. Schuller began his ministry with two members and five hundred dollars in a drive-in theater in California in 1955. In 1995, the world-famous Crystal Cathedral congregation celebrated its fortieth anniversary! Today, Dr. Schuller is seen and heard by more people each week than any other religious leader in the world. He is the founder and spokesman on America's television church, "The Hour of Power," which is the longest-running and most widely viewed weekly televised church service in America, and the first church service of its kind in Europe, Asia, Australia and Russia.

Dr. Schuller is the author of thirty books, five of which were on The New York Times *and* Publishers Weekly *best-seller lists.* Prayer: My Soul's Adventure with God *is his autobiography. His lifetime of actual involvement in architecture, psychology, theology, and motivational seminars makes him a true Renaissance man. He lives with his wife, Arvella, in Garden Grove, California.*

My Word!

Possible

It's possible. It is possible for me to name my favorite word. That word is **possible**.

Let anyone come up with a positive idea, suggestion, dream or plan, and if one confident, enthusiastic, intelligent person will open his mouth and say, "it's possible," immediately creative brain cells that have been lurking in the deep subconscious will be aroused, stirred and called to march into the conscious mind responding like dedicated workers to this stimulating word!

I have seen marriages headed for divorce court only to turn the corner toward reconciliation when someone said, "it's possible."

I have seen people headed for depressing, discouraging defeat until someone caused them to believe that they could succeed by simply telling them, "it's possible."

Nick Meglin

An editor of Mad *magazine for more than thirty years, Nick Meglin also is author of twelve books and more than a hundred magazine and newspaper articles that have appeared in, among others,* The New York Times Sunday News Magazine, Newsday, Tennis Magazine, Opera News, Quarterback, American Artist *and* Step-by-Step Graphics.

He majored in English and Psychology at Brooklyn College and completed his Bachelor of Fine Arts at the School of Visual Arts, where he majored in illustration. He also taught drawing and illustration at his alma mater's night school for more than ten years.

A member of ASCAP, Nick Meglin also belongs to the Writers Guild of America, the Dramatists Guild, the National Eagle Scout Association and the Society of Illustrators. He says he's also the president of the Tenacity Fan Club.

MY WORD!

Stick-to-itiveness

As an editor of *MAD* magazine, a man of letters I'm not. Maybe nine or ten, maybe, but I've never dealt with a full deck or full alphabet since my Stuyvesant High School days. In that erstwhile NYC learning academy, a fine young English teacher, Mr. Jarrow, had a passion for words that "said a lot with a little." His passion proved contagious, and most of us emerged from his class transformed. One of his favorites, and subsequently one of mine, was the word "tenacity." No one in the class could come up with a one-word trade-off, and the closest we came to it (albeit a hyphenated cheat) was **stick-to-itiveness**.

And that's my contribution.

If you've hung in with me this far, man, you've got tenacity! (That's a little shtick-to-itiveness . . . sorry!)

Frank Deford

Six times voted America's Sportswriter of the Year by his peers at the National Association of Sportscasters and Sportswriters, Frank Deford displayed another side of himself in his poignant book, Alex: The Life of a Child, *the touching memoir about his daughter who was a victim of Cystic Fibrosis. The book was made into a motion picture and received the Christopher Award. His other books include* Everybody's All-American, Big Bill Tilden, *and* Love and Infamy, *a story taking place just before Pearl Harbor.*

Frank Deford has been a contributing editor to Vanity Fair *magazine, sports columnist for National Public Radio and ESPN and correspondent for the HBO magazine show, "Realsport." The American Journalism Review has cited him as the nation's Best Sportswriter and, on two occasions, he has been honored as Magazine Writer of the Year by the Washington Journalism Review. In broadcasting, he has been a weekly regular on NPR's "Morning Edition" since 1980 and, in 1988, he was awarded an Emmy for his work on NBC at the Seoul Olympic Games.*

A native of Baltimore and a 1962 graduate of Princeton, he lives in Westport, Connecticut, with his wife, Carol.

Now

It's too easy to select a warm and fuzzy word like love or mother or America or beer, but I prefer a tougher word that has more punch to it. I would choose **now**.

Now is good because it isn't ambiguous. It is also very important. Even if you like to live in the past or plan for the future, now matters a great deal, because someday the past will be what's now, and if you want to enjoy the past you have to take care of now. And if you don't attend to things now, your future won't be worth much.

But now isn't just now. If you use now as an interjective, it really means business. When you hear somebody say, "Now, here's the plan," you know it's going to be a whale of a plan.

Also, no word in the world, in any language, carries such authority as now does when spoken by an authority figure, like your mother or your teacher or your boss, especially after you have said, "I'll do it later."

Now is a very unsung word that deserves great honor, especially since it is also neat and short and easy to spell.

Patricia Nixon

Born as Thelma Catherine Ryan in Ely, Nevada, on the day before St. Patrick's Day, this former First Lady chose to be called "Pat." She recalled that "Patricia was my father's favorite name. I was his 'St. Patrick's Babe in the morning'."

She worked to put herself through the University of Southern California and served as a high school teacher prior to meeting and marrying a young Whittier attorney named Richard Nixon in 1940.

Mrs. Nixon became her husband's partner in races for Congress, the Senate, the Vice Presidency and the White House. In public life, she saw all the wonders of America and the world, and she touched millions of hearts with her infinite and special grace.

Her work in the White House flowed from her boundless compassion for humanity. She was the first First Lady to champion volunteerism. She blazed the literacy trail with her Right to Read program. She pushed to establish new recreational areas in or near big cities for those who could not afford to visit distant national parks.

In retirement, Mrs. Nixon was a devoted grandmother to Jennie, Christopher, Alex Richard and Melanie. Although she kept her public appearances to a minimum, polls show she remained one of America's most admired women. The First Lady who spoke the language of the heart still touches the heart of America.

MY WORD!

Caring

To choose one word to include in a lexicon is as challenging as choosing one book to be stranded with on a desert island! The word I would select, however, is one which encompasses our minds and hearts and our actions: **caring**.

The course of our lives is affected by caring, our caring for others, the use of our time, our environment, our way of life, our goals and priorities. It gives purpose and meaning to our individual lives. Through caring, compassion and concern are translated into the commitment to act for the betterment of our fellow man and the preservation, perpetuation or improvement of all we deem vital.

Caring creates the spirit and determines the destiny of a nation.

Carl Karcher

A native of Upper Sandusky, Ohio, Carl Karcher headed west at the age of twenty to work in his uncle's feed store in Anaheim, California, for eighteen dollars a week. Two years later, he was hired as a bread wrapper by a Los Angeles bakery and quickly promoted to sales and delivery. In July of 1941, he purchased a hot dog cart for $326 ($15 cash and $311 borrowed on his 1941 Plymouth). First day sales totaled $14.75.

By 1995, that hot dog cart had grown to more than 650 Carl's Jr. Restaurants located in California, Arizona, Nevada, Oregon, Utah, Mexico and Maylasia. Carl's Jr. Restaurants are owned and operated, franchised or licensed by Carl Karcher Enterprises, Inc., which employs approximately eleven thousand people.

He is an active supporter and board member of many non-profit groups and encourages his employees to be involved in the community as well. He is the recipient of the Horatio Alger Award, the Private Enterprise Exemplar Medal from the Freedoms Foundation at Valley Forge, and the Americanism Award from the Boy Scouts of America. He has been Knighted into the Order of Malta, one of the highest honors a layperson of the Catholic Church can attain. He served on the Grace Commission to identify waste and inefficiency in government.

Family

If I had to choose one word in the English language that was more significant to me than any other in the dictionary, that word would have to be **family**. I have enjoyed all kinds of blessings and good fortune in my life, but without a family with whom to share the laughter and the joys—as well as the challenges and the tears—my life would not be as meaningful.

First there was my family of origin—a loving mother and father, six brothers and a sister—which instilled in me the values I have held so dear all my life. These include a strong sense of right and wrong, the importance of religious conviction, the value of hard work and the perseverance to reach for my dreams no matter what barriers were placed in my way.

Then, of course, there is the family I created with my wonderful wife, Margaret. I believe that a strong marriage is the foundation for the family values that get so much lip service today—and for more than fifty-five years, my beautiful bride has stood beside me. She is the mother of our 12 children, and our large extended family now includes 47 grandchildren and 12 great-grandchildren.

With Margaret's faith and trust always supporting me, I was able to set goals and follow my strong ambitions to build another family of sorts—a family of fast-food restaurants that, in turn, has spawned a family of dedicated employees that can be credited for much of the growth and success of our company.

Yes, I have a very strong belief in the family—and I emphatically agree that as the family goes, so goes the nation.

Stephen King

Photo by Tabitha King

As TIME *magazine put it, Stephen King is "the indisputable King of horror." His novels, screenplays and short stories combine a prolific blend of fantasy, speculative fiction and terror into a consistently scary brew. From his initial successful novel,* Carrie, *published in 1974, his gruesomely entertaining books continue to sell millions and top the best-seller lists. He's published almost thirty books under two names, along with screenplays and novellas that inspired additional motion picture adaptations.*

He alludes to Howard Phillips Lovecraft in his contribution of a favorite word, paying homage to the writer many consider the father of the modern horror genre. King writes of a truly tenebrific world, as did Lovecraft, in which mysterious monsters, supernatural creatures and disembodied spirits roam. His flesh-creeping books include Pet Sematary, Firestarter, It, Misery, The Dark Half, Four Past Midnight, Gerald's Game, Dolores Claiborne *and* Needful Things.

Tenebrous

Thanks for inquiring about my favorite word. I like **tenebrous**, have no idea what it really means, but it sounds incredibly ookey, and Lovecraft used it a lot. I really like it.

Herbert D. Eagle

One of the great proponents of the gentle art of salesmanship was Herbert. D. Eagle. He served as the long-time president of Sales and Marketing Executives International while Vice President of Marketing for Transamerica Corporation and Senior Vice President of International Programs for Occidental Life Insurance Company of California.

Sell

One word has been a source of irritation to me—not because I don't like it, but because of its misuse. That word is **sell**.

All the dictionaries I have examined define sell essentially in anachronistic or pejorative terms. For example, I found, in consulting what everyone considers to be the best known dictionary, that the definition begins thus: *to deliver or give up in violation of duty, trust or loyalty: Betray.* It goes on with, *to give up in return for something else esp. foolishly or dishonorably . . .to deliver into slavery for money—to give into the power of another—to dispose of or manage for profit instead of in accordance with conscience, justice or duty—to impose upon: Cheat —a deliberate deception: Hoax.*

If I had the authority to change the definition of this word, I would say, "to assist (a consumer) in the intelligent use of his purchasing power by truthfully presenting the best and most appropriate values to meet his needs." The old English verb, "sellan," from which sell is derived, means "to give, to deliver." It is my hope that this little word will gain the stature it truly deserves. After all, nothing really happens until somebody sells something.

Dr. Bernie Siegel

Dr. Bernie Siegel

Bernard S. Siegel, M.D., prefers to be called Bernie, not Dr. Siegel. He is a graduate of Colgate University and the Cornell University Medical School. He practices as a pediatric and general surgeon in New Haven, Connecticut, and is the man who, more than fifteen years ago, began talking about patient empowerment and the choices one has to live fully and to die in peace.

As a physician who has cared for and counseled thousands of patients with life-threatening illnesses, Dr. Siegel embraces a philosophy of living and dying that stands at the forefront of the medical ethics issues with which modern society grapples. Just as his two previous best-selling books, Love, Medicine & Miracles *and* Peace, Love & Healing, *broke new ground in the art of healing, the third of his ever-popular inspirational books,* How to Live Between Office Visits: A Guide to Life, Love & Health, *promises to add to his stature as one of America's greatest humanizers of medical education.*

Love

My favorite word is **love**. What the world needs now and forever is love.

Faith, hope and love but the greatest of these is love. . . .

Love cures diseases. Love heals physical and emotional wounds. Love is the greatest survival mechanism known to man.

Religions are started by lovers and destroyed by rule makers. So instead of leading to more love, they lead to war and death.

If we were all to act as loving mothers toward one another, there would be no reason to fear for our planet's future.

Love one another. Love thine enemies. Love yourself.

Self-love is not related to selfishness or self-interest but is necessary if one is to love others.

When it comes time to introduce yourself to God, I hope you will realize you don't need an introduction.

I think we should all have our baby pictures on licenses and identification cards so everyone will see we are lovable.

If ever in doubt, remember to love yourself as you would your pet. If we all did so, we would be far less self-destructive.

I am starting the ASPCH. Like the ASPCA, it will shelter, feed and love humans instead of animals. So, if you lack love in your life, come to our arms for shelter.

Danny Cox

Danny Cox, accelerationist, provides fast-paced, humorous and informative presentations designed to give step-by-step guidance on how to break barriers in leadership, personal performance and customer service. From years of flying supersonic fighters as an air show and test pilot to years of breaking records in the business world with an eight hundred percent increase in production from the district he lead, Danny puts real world techniques in each of his skill-building, thought-provoking sessions.

Danny is the author of two best-selling books, Leadership When the Heat's On, *and* Seize the Day: 7 Steps to Achieving the Extraordinary in an Ordinary World. *As testimony to his professionalism, he holds the Council of Peers Award for Excellence, a designation awarded to less than three percent of the thirty-two hundred member National Speakers Association. Danny is also a member of the elite Speakers Roundtable, a group of twenty professionals who are dedicated to speaking excellence.*

Adventure

The word I choose above all others is **adventure**.

I fell in love with it first as a spectator while I was growing up in Marion, Illinois, during World War II. My adventure-filled weekends consisted of a trip to each of the town's two movie theaters to see the latest John Wayne, Roy Rogers or Gene Autry movie. That was in the days when heroes were truly good guys.

Later on in college I became more of a participant in adventure. One of the part-time jobs I had then was mapping and exploring caves, which was certainly the ultimate adventure, or so I thought. But that wasn't the case.

After graduation, I spent ten years flying supersonic fighters. My first time through the sound barrier was from forty-three hundred feet in a vertical dive at full throttle, in afterburner, pointed directly at the Okefenokee Swamp. That was an adventure, but there were bigger ones to follow. Later I was flying airplanes at almost twice the speed of sound; airplanes that could go supersonic in a climb. An exciting adventure but not the ultimate.

After leaving the Air Force, I thought my quest for real adventure was over. Wrong again, it was just starting.

I was a salesperson for a year with a large sales company

Danny Cox (continued)

when I was made manager of one of their small offices. A year later they promoted me to manager of the top office out of their thirty-six offices. In just three months time, I totally destroyed the office because I was trying to turn my salespeople into copies of me. They didn't want to be copies of me. Can you imagine that? My boss told me he was looking for my replacement. The ultimate adventure had begun. By going to work on me and not my co-workers, we rebuilt the office back to number one, and an industry leader.

This is what I learned from experience. The ultimate adventure lies just across the threshold that marks the boundary between our developed and undeveloped potential. And with discipline we can have a little of that ultimate adventure every day!

Mary Kay Ash

Mary Kay Ash is the American entrepreneur who parlayed her cosmetics line to a major position on the stock market through direct marketing and home contacts. Mary Kay Cosmetics has grown since its founding in 1963 to a company with annual sales surpassing one billion dollars.

The firm has been listed on the Fortune 500 register of the nation's top industrial companies. Each year new sales records are set as hundreds of thousands of Mary Kay beauty consultants in more than twenty countries are successful in merchandising their products. Pink may be the color of the Cadillacs given to leading Mary Kay sales associates as rewards for their efforts, and pink may be the color of the company's stationery, but green is the color of the money that has made Chairman Emeritus Mary Kay Ash a wealthy and respected marketing genius.

You can!

Our young people today seem to be filled with negativity and doubt. I delight in admonishing them that they can do anything in this world they want to do—if they want to do it badly enough and are willing to pay the price. My favorite words are **you can**!

Lawrence Welk

Certainly one of the most popular and durable band leaders, Lawrence Welk was born in Strasburg, North Dakota. His ability to adapt to ever-changing musical tastes served him well until his death in 1992. Early in his career, he developed a sweet-sounding style he termed "champagne music," and made it his signature throughout a career that took him from one-night stands in the Midwest to weekly syndicated TV programs.

His shows featured a combination of ragtime piano, tap dancing, ballroom dancing, vocal groups, polkas and whatever he imagined would please his audiences. To oversee his many activities, he formed Teleklew Productions and developed a resort in Southern California with adjacent playhouse and golf course that remains a monument to his popularity.

MY WORD!

Wonderful

I guess I've gotten more mileage out of the word **wonderful** than anyone in history. I've become so closely identified with this word that impressionists (both professional and amateur) need only say "wonderful, wonderful" with a slight accent to receive credit for a perfect Lawrence Welk impersonation.

Sometimes it seems that I regard this word as my personal property. When someone in my presence uses the word, I am often tempted to say, "Wait a minute, you're stealing MY WORD!"

When I wrote my autobiography in 1971, the publishers insisted on using the word for the title, (repeated, and spelled as they tell me I pronounce it)—*Wunnerful, Wunnerful!*

Perhaps I do use this word too frequently, and in some instances a trifle loosely. But as a North Dakota farm boy, and a grade-school drop-out, I hope I'll be excused for my limited vocabulary. And after all, considering my many blessings—my devoted family, my talented musical family, and our army of loyal fans, it's really not surprising that, to me, everything is wonderful—pardon me—wunnerful, wunnerful!

General Robinson Risner

Photo Courtesy of U.S. Air Force

Fighter pilot Robinson Risner spent seven of the prime years of his life as a prisoner of the North Vietnamese, most of the time locked in a cramped, cage-like cell. His period of confinement, between frequent sessions of interrogation and torture, provided him with an unusual opportunity to contemplate life and the circumstances with which he was faced. After his release following the halt of hostilities, he was assigned by the United States Air Force as Commander of an Air Fighter Division. His experiences led to the writing of a powerful accounting of his ordeal in an inspiring volume titled, The Passing of the Night. *His likeness was featured on the cover of TIME magazine on April 23, 1965, and again in that periodical in a retrospective of the Vietnam War thirty years later. He retired from the Air Force in 1976 as a Brigadier General.*

He then organized and chaired the Texas War on Drugs with Ross Perot, said to be the world's major effort of its kind, and now lives in Austin, Texas.

Faith

I awake each morning with **faith** that the day will provide a challenge to fill my day with endeavor; accomplishment enough to bring contentment and plenty of love to bring happiness.

Faith in myself gives me the courage of my convictions.

Faith in others provides me with tolerance, understanding and trust.

Faith in God is a constant source of strength and comfort.

And faith in country gives such pride.

Faith in these things has proven to be an unbeatable combination.

Tom Landry — Persistent

Tom Landry

Texas-born Tom Landry made a name for himself as a top defensive back with the New York Giants. He was the first head coach of the NFL's Dallas Cowboys and served in that capacity for 29 seasons, winning 18 division titles and 2 of 5 Super Bowls in which they appeared. His motivational and inspirational abilities make him a popular platform speaker.

Persistent

Words, to me, must come alive to have real meaning. In the world of professional football we talk in terms of competitiveness, aggressiveness, toughness—all "action" words. When we describe an athlete, we talk in terms of agility, quickness, balance or coordination—again, "action" words. However, if I had to single out one word that would mean most to me, it would be **persistent**. Persistence in athletics has more to do with success than any other trait. The dictionary says persistence is "to go on resolutely or stubbornly in spite of difficulties." A star athlete must have talent, skill and dedication, but most of all, he must be persistent.

MY WORD!

Dr. Paul Popenoe

For many years, the American Institute of Family Relations was one of the first organizations of its kind to focus on preserving marriages in a nation in which divorces were almost endemic. Dr. Paul Popenoe founded the Institute and served for many years as its Chairman of the Board.

Love

Being concerned with almost every aspect of marriage and family life, I have encountered the word **love** frequently. But I must admit that I cannot tell what it means. It does not mean the same to any two persons and it means all sorts of different things to the same person. For example, an old hillbilly song declares, "I love my wife, I love my baby, I love my biscuits dipped in gravy." Apparently they are all on the same level to him.

It means one thing in church on Sunday, perhaps something entirely different on Monday.

It is often said to be the most beautiful word in the language, yet a Los Angeles newspaper, describing a particularly vicious rape of a woman by a stranger who broke into her home, described him in the headline as a "love burglar."

Inevitably, much damage results from the use of a word that has so many meanings that it ends by having none at all!

No later than junior high school, we ought to devote a considerable amount of time to analyzing this word and identifying (if that's possible) its many meanings. If that is an impossible task, perhaps we ought to start a movement to have it taken out of the dictionary, replacing it with some more definite form of speech.

Meanwhile, I don't undertake to settle the question, "What is love?" for anyone else. Whenever it is used in your presence, find out for yourself before you go any farther.

Admiral Elmo R. Zumwalt, Jr.

Elmo Zumwalt joined the United States Navy in 1942, and commanded the United States Naval forces in Vietnam from 1968 to 1970. He was promoted to the rank of Chief of Naval Operations following this tour of duty and earned fame for his "Z-grams." These communications were in the form of personal orders generated by his desire to improve relationships among the races while modernizing personnel matters. His son, Elmo Zumwalt III, was exposed to Agent Orange while serving in Vietnam, and collaborated with Admiral Zumwalt in a book entitled My Father, My Son.

Communications

My favorite word has always been **communications**—the ability to make one's thoughts, ideas and self known to everyone, both far and near. It has been my favorite for over thirty years, ever since my high school days in California.

Being Valedictorian of my class, on the debate teams in high school and at the Naval Academy, Commanding Officer of U.S. Navy ships and, finally, as Chief of Naval Operations, has taught me the need for communication and the ability to communicate.

In my capacity as CNO, I tried to communicate to senior officers, as well as to junior enlisted men, the need for two-way communication. It is necessary in the military environment — as well as the civilian domain—in order to have a closely knit organization, doing its job as best it can, whenever called upon.

This ability to communicate with others is needed in all walks of life if one is to be successful. Without communication, things may go wrong and affect one's ability to carry out assigned tasks. Without it, how could the urgency or importance, or need for a job be conveyed or understood? In closing, communication is the catalyst needed if individuals, groups or nations are to come together for the betterment of themselves.

Father Theodore Hesburgh

This noted religious leader's career at Notre Dame University culminated with his selection as president in 1952, a role in which he served until his retirement in 1987. During his term as president, Father Hesburgh secularized and integrated the university and was instrumental in encouraging the athletic department to accept greater administrative controls. He also was a charter member of the United States Civil Rights Commission.

Civility

Civility is a great word and is one of the great civic virtues. In fact, it is the basic civic virtue if men are to live together in peace and harmony. It means, first of all, that everyone treats each other with the dignity that befits us as human beings, brothers, sons of God. It means that we can disagree with each other without shouting at each other. It means that we can take different sides of a question, discuss it amiably and forcefully, and remain friends, even though the disagreement remains as well. Civility is absolutely necessary in a pluralistic society with many cultures, many races, many religions, and many different kinds of people. Civility is what makes our country a comity instead of a jungle.

Meredith Willson

Born in Mason City, Iowa, this noted composer and lyricist once toured with the John Philip Sousa band. He was the principal flutist with the New York Philharmonic Symphony Orchestra and later became the musical director of many popular radio programs.

He composed scores for the motion pictures and wrote the hit song, "May the Good Lord Bless and Keep You." Perhaps his greatest success came with his musical play, The Music Man, *with the unforgettable "76 Trombones" and "Marian the Librarian." He composed both the lyrics and music for this as well as for his later hit,* The Unsinkable Molly Brown.

Rosemary

"Flower" ought to be a beautiful word in view of its meaning—but look at yourself in the mirror pronouncing it and—well, just try it.

"Cake" should be attractive too, but it is probably the edgiest word in the dictionary—so blasted crackley.

"Beautiful" is sonically ugly also; and uglier to see—to watch the formations of one's mouth during the process of its enunciation. (Try it slowly—really meaning it.)

No, I haven't enunciated every word in the dictionary on a test basis—but I am completely satisfied (applying sonic, visual, oral and aesthetics standards) with **rosemary**. I held that opinion, by the way, years before I ever met a girl of that name, let alone married her.

Jimmy Dean

As Chairman of the Board of Directors of Jimmy Dean Foods, a Division of the Sara Lee Corporation, Jimmy Dean enjoys all the privileges of successful entrepreneurship. His Jimmy Dean Sausages grace the breakfast tables of millions of Americans, some of whom aren't familiar with his prior status as an entertainer responsible for the sales of millions of recordings.

This six-foot-three native of Plainview, Texas, took the Nashville Country and Western scene by storm with his renditions of such songs as "Big Bad John," "The First Thing Ev'ry Morning (And the Last Thing Ev'ry Night)," "The Farmer and the Lord," "Sixteen Tons," and "Chattanoogie Shoeshine Boy." But it was his frequent guest appearances on "The Tonight Show" filling in for Johnny Carson that his self-effacing humor, and his all-around good nature made him one of the biggest and brightest stars of Columbia Records.

He now gives that same energy, dedication and enthusiasm to his business interests.

Tenacity

In response to your request, my favorite word is **tenacity**. I learned what the word meant from my mother. Although she never used the word, she taught me that you never give up. And through her teachings and efforts, I was endowed with a considerable amount of tenacity. Her teachings have indeed been a blessing throughout the years.

I certainly know the meaning of the word tenacity. I have kept the word defeat, as best I could, from entering into my vocabulary. As I once said, you can't change the direction of the wind, but you can adjust your sails and reach your destination.

Here of late, I see far too little tenacity. Being knocked down is part of life; getting up is also. And, God knows, I have been knocked down a lot of times, but so far I have always gotten up.

Tenacity. I still can't spell it.

Robert Mondavi

Robert Mondavi continues his active schedule as wine's foremost spokesperson even in his eighties. A native of Virginia, Minnesota, he learned the skills of producing, vinifying and marketing wines at an early age, working with his father, Cesare, before graduating from Stanford University in 1936. In 1943, he convinced his father to purchase the Charles Krug Winery and began a lifelong career of innovation and experimentation. He singlehandedly popularized new styles of wine and methods of fermentation. He traveled to Europe to study Old World techniques. In 1966, he built the Robert Mondavi Winery, an ongoing monument to his dreams.

He is a founding co-chairman with Julia Child of the American Institute of Wine and Food, a member of the American Wine Society and its Winemaker of the Year in 1982. He has served as president of the International Wine and Spirits Competition of London, and serves in the Advisory Council of the American Conference of Chefs. He and his wife, Margrit Biever, now spend much of their time traveling, promoting both the wines of California and the Robert Mondavi Winery and working to assure the proper understanding of wine in cultures throughout the world.

MY WORD!

Excel

My favorite word is **excel**.

From my parents I learned that the family had a commitment to excel in whatever we were doing. When the family went into wine-growing, it was a small, family-oriented business without much science or investment,

I knew we had to excel. We had the grapes, the climate and the soil in Napa Valley, and we began to aim at the French wines, which were at that time known as the best. It took us decades to do it, but we have finally arrived.

Now, when I talk to groups around the world, I tell them that they can excel in whatever area they choose, and that the rewards are both personal and professional.

Letitia Baldrige

A graduate of Vassar College, Letitia Baldrige is the recipient of four honorary degrees (Doctors of Humane Letters.) She served as Social Secretary to Ambassador and Mrs. David Bruce at the American Embassy in Paris, then became the special assistant to Ambassador Clare Boothe Luce at the embassy in Rome. During the John F. Kennedy administration, she was Chief of Staff for Mrs. Kennedy and Social Secretary to the White House. Subsequently, she served as an advisor to four First Ladies.

In 1964 she opened Letitia Baldrige Enterprises, Inc., which provides management training in the field of behavior. She lectures and produces seminars for companies throughout the United States and abroad. She was the cover subject of TIME magazine in an issue devoted to America's manners.

Her thirteenth book, Letitia Baldrige's New Complete Guide to Executive Manners, has been translated and published in several other languages. She is a contributing editor of Town & Country magazine and writes a weekly syndicated newspaper column, "RSVP," for the Copley News Service as well as a monthly column for New Choices magazine.

Mesmerize

The dictionaries define **mesmerize** in terms of hypnotizing, spellbinding, fascinating, etc., but dictionaries don't provide any of the romance of certain words.

I love words that are sensuous, and mesmerize is impossible to say without its sounding sensuous. The word even looks beautiful on the page. It is affirmatively attractive in its meaning, too. When you tell people you have been mesmerized by something, they start to smile. They're affected by the word; it has a contagious, happy ring to it.

In my youth, I was constantly falling in love and was always being mesmerized by the man in question and by life in general. Today I am still serendipitously mesmerized by a snatch of a song, a sight of a glorious painting, a glimpse of a fresh green fern growing from the crack of an ancient monument, and the taste of an incredible wine. I guess the word mesmerize describes a state of happiness, or the memory of a state of happiness, which is just as good!

Michael Crichton

Michael Crichton began writing plays in the third grade, sold his first article to The New York Times *at fourteen and completed his first bestseller,* The Andromeda Strain, *while a student at Harvard Medical School. Among his other popular books and motion pictures are* The Terminal Man, The Great Train Robbery, Coma, Westworld, Looker, Runaway, Physical Evidence *and the most popular movie of all time,* Jurassic Park. *He followed this blockbuster novel with a sequel titled* The Lost World *published by Knopf and extending his earlier tale of bioengineered dinosaur DNA gone wild. In 1995, his creation, the NBC medical series "ER," was nominated for 23 Emmy Awards and won 8. It is said to be based on his experiences as a medical student.*

At 6 ft. 9 in., he may be the tallest American author to turn his novels to box office gold. This Chicago native's passion for science, art, technology and entertainment has led to burgeoning book and movie ticket sales. TIME magazine, in a cover feature on Crichton, described him as "one of those high-end, abstract thinking machines." His contribution to this volume projects this image.

Symbol

I am particularly fond of the word **symbol** since it represents the most complex of abstract thoughts. That is, all words are symbols, but uniquely the word symbol refers to the idea of such abstractions and not to any particular abstraction.

It is probably true that my preference for the word symbol in itself symbolizes something about the symbolic uses to which I put language; then again, it may only mean that I am one of those people who likes to be confused and spends a lot of time making sure that he is. I could go on talking about symbols indefinitely, but probably I should stop here before I become incoherent, a state characterized, among other things, by an inability to convey clearly the symbolic content of thought and speech patterns.

In stopping, I'm sure that the reader and I can both share a small sigh of relief.

Jack Kemp

A native of Los Angeles and a graduate of Occidental College, Jack Kemp spent 13 years as a professional football quarterback. He was elected captain of the San Diego Chargers from 1960 to 1962 and of the Buffalo Bills, a team he helped lead to the AFL championship in 1964 and 1965, when he was named the league's Most Valuable Player. He co-founded the AFL Players Association and was five times elected president.

He came to the United States Congress in 1971 and represented the Buffalo area and western New York for nine terms in the House of Representatives. Prior to founding Empower America in 1993, he served for four years as U.S. Secretary of Housing and Urban Development, and proved to be one of our nation's most innovative leaders in that role. Empower America is dedicated to three founding principles: expanding freedom and democratic capitalism around the world; promoting policies to expand economic growth, job creation, and entrepreneurship for our nation; and advancing social policies which empower people, not government bureaucracies.

In January 1995, Jack Kemp announced that he would not seek the Republican presidential nomination in 1996. He said at the time that his passion for ideas was not matched by a passion for fundraising.

Idea

The power of ideas has been the guiding force of civilization. Philosophy, including Platonic, Hegelian, and Kantian, recognizes **idea** as the supreme principle. Because ideas reign supreme in a free society, idea is my favorite word.

This page and this book are manifestations of real thoughts, which are called ideas. Ideas are the real thoughts to which all perceived reality is compared. Therefore, ideas are all; they are infinite, and as such, are the underpinnings of all that we seem, do, think and feel.

I enjoyed professional football, but I love the competition of ideas even more. Ideas rule the world, for good or bad, and in an arena so powerful there can be no spectators. Ideas govern man; by transcending time, distance, race, and other dimensions of society, they have charted the course of history.

Politics is the experience of idea, discovery, debate, change, institution and rejection. In politics, we attempt to persuade others of the rightness of our ideas. Those ideas which are rightly conceived, thoughtfully presented, honestly intended and which strike responsive chords in the minds of others, mark the course of nations and yes, the world.

No thing, no word, could do or be greater than that.

Dave Barry

Dave Barry was born in Armonk, New York, in 1947 and claims he has been steadily growing older ever since without ever having reached maturity. He attended public schools, and says he is proud to have been elected class clown. He graduated from Haverford College where he (in his words) "eventually got a job with a local newspaper named—this is a real name — the Daily Local News, in West Chester, Pa., and covered a series of incredibly dull municipal meetings, some of which are still going on."

He moved on to join Burger Associates, a consulting firm that had as its goal the teaching of effective writing to business people. In 1983, he began his tenure with the Miami Herald, *leading to a Pulitzer Prize in 1988 for commentary, again in his words, "pending a recount."*

His column appears in several hundred newspapers, and his books include Babies and Other Hazards of Sex, Dave Barry Slept Here: A Sort of History of the United States, Dave Barry's Complete Guide to Guys *and* Dave Barry Turns 40. *The CBS television series "Dave's World" is based on two of Barry's books.*

In addition, he says he owns a guitar that once was played by Bruce Springsteen.

Weasel

I've learned certain fundamental truths about humor. One of them is that **weasel** is a funny word. You can improve the humor value of almost any situation by injecting a weasel into it:

WRONG: "Scientists have discovered a twenty-third moon orbiting Jupiter."

RIGHT: "Scientists have discovered a giant weasel orbiting Jupiter."

WRONG: "U.S. Rep. Newt Gingrich."

RIGHT: "U.S. Rep. Weasel Gingrich."

Kate White

Kate White is the editor-in-chief of Redbook *magazine. She also is the author of the bestselling book,* Why Good Girls Don't Get Ahead . . . But Gutsy Girls Do. *She began her magazine career at* Glamour *as an editorial assistant after winning the magazine's Top Ten College Women contest. In 1993, Kate White was elected to the YMCA Academy of Women Achievers and received the Komen Foundation for Breast Cancer Award for Media. In 1994 she was named to the National Board of Distinguished Women by Mississippi University for Women.*

Wow

My favorite word is **Wow**. In my field, creativity is what matters, and when someone on my staff has an idea that makes me say wow it not only means we're probably having a great time, but that we're doing our jobs right. There are certain issues of the magazine that make me say wow, to myself over and over, and those are always the ones that rate highest with readers. As an author, I also know that if something I've written makes me think wow it's probably something that my editor will like too.

Mary Renault

Born in London where her father was a doctor, Mary Renault attended Oxford with the thought of becoming a teacher, but instead embarked on a career as a writer. Her first published novel was titled, Promise of Love. *She wrote three books during World War II while she was serving as a nurse. One of them,* Return to Night, *was the recipient of the MGM Award. Her travels in Greece while a resident of South Africa resulted in her brilliant reconstructions of ancient Hellas.* The Last of the Wine, The King Must Die, The Bull from the Sea, The Mask of Apollo *and others made her a world-renowned literary figure.*

No Favorites

My reaction to this query for a favourite word is immediate and strongly negative. No serious writer ought to have a favourite word. The value of words is determined by their settings, as with gems. One woman can wear a fistful of diamonds and look merely vulgar; another, who has spent her money on a Cellini pendant, will have a blister pearl of little intrinsic value shaped into a priceless work of art.

The first duty of a writer or anyone else is not to debase good words. "Glamour" was a magically evocative word in the early decades of this century in the hands of artists such as De la Mare. Now it types third-rate actresses. "Charisma" is going the same way. "Disinterested" in the sense of "not motivated by self-interest" is an important moral concept. Its use in place of "uninterested" has damaged thought as well as language.

The best words should be used the most seldom, and always to the maximum effect. Clichés are a major factor in the new barbarism.

Malcolm Boyd

Pastor of St. Augustine by the Sea Episcopal Church in Santa Monica, California, Malcolm Boyd is known as a social activist and frequent contributor to Modern Maturity *and other periodicals. He's the author of twenty-seven books, including the bestseller,* Are You Running With Me, Jesus?, *as well as* Take Off the Masks, *and* Rich with Years: Daily Meditations on Growing Older.

Boyd has been a civil rights and peace activist, a playwright, a Fellow at Yale, a performing artist and a film critic. He has served for three terms as president of PEN Center USA West, a branch of the international association of writers. His archive, a permanent collection of his letters and papers, is at Boston University. He is chaplain of the AIDS Commission of the Episcopal Diocese of Los Angeles.

We

I cannot choose my favorite word anymore than I can cite my favorite opera, vegetable or book. Yet there is a word that I consider highly significant and a favorite because it holds intense personal meaning for me.

It is **we**. It softens the solitary, strident egotism of "I." It enables any human, loving, friendly, working relationship where we becomes salvific; true bonding knows the meaning of sacrifice, compromise, collegiality, and mutuality. Too, it opens up a dialogue with God in the form of prayer or meditation. When I address "Thou," "You" or "the Other," the conversation inescapably takes on the equation of "we."

Living as we do in the global village, where the whole world comes together in intricate networking, the word "we" characterizes our experience. We serves as a model and an ideal and a warning: Ask not for whom the bell tolls — it tolls for you and me.

Chuck Jonak

Chuck
Jonak

Chuck Jonak, managing editor of Kiwanis *magazine in Indianapolis, Indiana, is a native of Chicago, where he began his journalism career on the staffs of several suburban newspapers. After receiving his master's degree in journalism from Northern Illinois University at DeKalb in 1980, he joined Kiwanis International as an assistant editor. In 1989 he served as editor of the Kiwanis history book,* Dimensions of Service, *and in 1990,* Kiwanis *received The American Society of Journalists and Authors Outstanding Magazine Award under his leadership.*

Righteous

I first heard the word when I was eight or nine years old. My brother was playing a "single," and the powerful ending of the song caught my ear: "Bring back that loving feeling, oh that loving feeling . . . ." I asked him who was singing, and he told me The Righteous Brothers.

It strikes me as odd that the word **righteous** rarely seems to appear in print or, for that matter, in speech. It's a shame really, because it is a strong and noble word with deep-rooted meaning for the human experience.

To be virtuous. To believe in a justifiable cause. To rise up and stand resolutely opposed to that which is clearly reprehensible. These are intrinsic to human behavior in a moral society, but righteousness appears to be a gray concept today.

Yes, that is a shame. And it certainly isn't righteous.

Tom Harmon

Tom Harmon

All-American running back at the University of Michigan, Tom Harmon is perhaps the most famous athlete to graduate from Horace Mann High School in Gary, Indiana. He won the 1940 Heisman Trophy as the nation's outstanding college football player before enlisting in the Army Air Corps. After surviving two airplane crashes, he earned the Silver Star and Purple Heart Medals. He then returned to football as a halfback with the Los Angeles Rams. He began a new career as a radio and television sports broadcaster following his retirement from football, and enjoyed many years in that capacity, covering numerous athletic events from coast to coast.

MY WORD!

Humility

If I had to pick a favorite word, I think that word would be **humility**.

The word has been the most descriptive characteristic of almost every famous person I have met. Realizing this point, I invariably go back in my memory to my mother and a most valuable lesson she taught me as a freshman in high school. I had just come from the high school practice field where I had managed to run through the varsity for three touchdowns. I was all puffed up and explaining in detail to a couple of my pals what I had accomplished.

When my friends left, my mother took me aside and said, "Tom, I am very proud of you. I think you are going to accomplish much in this world. But I would be much happier if you allowed others to speak of your accomplishments. If you are good enough, you won't have to blow your own horn, others will do it for you."

I don't think that I have ever forgotten that lesson. I know that I will be forever thankful that I had a mother who passed on to me one of the most valuable lessons of my life. Humility is one thing I admire most in a person.

Stephen Ambrose

Boyd professor of history at The University of New Orleans, Stephen Ambrose is the author of the best-seller D-Day: June 6, 1944: the Climactic Battle, *telling how World War II reshaped the future of the United States. He is the editor of the two-volume* Eisenhower Papers *as well as a number of other books dealing with history and military affairs.*

Among his better-known books are Rise to Globalism: American Foreign Policy 1938-1970; Crazy Horse and Custer: The Parallel Lives of Two American Warriors; Duty, Honor, Country: A History of West Point *and the three-volume work titled* Nixon: The Education of a Politician 1913-1962. *His definitive works are known for their exhaustive research and balance.*

Duty

My favorite word is **duty**.

It is a powerful word that brings together and sums up such ideas as responsibility, honor, character and trust. Duty compels us to meet our obligations to our fellow man. It forces us to do more than speak about what needs to be done for the common good, but to act on it.

Duty was Robert E. Lee's favorite English word. Also Dwight D. Eisenhower's.

My least favorite word is tragedy. Not because of the word itself—it too is a powerful word—but because of the way it is misused, especially by the media. Every automobile accident is a tragedy nowadays, indeed virtually every violent death is described as a tragedy. This misuse robs the word of its force—not to mention its meaning.

Fletcher Knebel

Photo by Thomas McGrath

A Dayton, Ohio, native, Fletcher Knebel worked from 1937 to 1964 as a Washington correspondent for a number of newspapers and periodicals. As a daily columnist in the nation's capital, he had first-hand knowledge of the inner workings of the government. This led to his writing several best-selling novels including No High Ground, The Bottom Line, Seven Days in May, Night of Camp David, Vanished *and* Trespass.

As president of Washington's Gridiron Club, he was active in many behind-the-scenes political activities. This graduate of Miami University in Oxford, Ohio, later served as a staff writer for Look *magazine.*

A careful examination of current dictionaries fails to reveal the exact definition of his contribution of a favorite word.

MY WORD!

Thridge

Thridge!
The word has everything. It floats on the valley breeze, misted with nostalgia, brushed by the wings of night birds and dipped in the blood-red shadows of a thousand ghostly camp fires. Thridge says it all. It speaks of alienation, of Dr. Spock, affection, camphor, lengthy legal suits, of Boise, Idaho, of acupuncture, long nights of love, Jeb Magruder, the Kansas City Chiefs and inevitably, of the decline of the West.

Thridge is a sturdy, purposeful word. It stands solidly on its five consonants and two vowels, gazing across a purple mesa at a lowering sun. Thridge brims with motivation, with goals, yet retains withal a soupçon of mystery, a dash of the raffish.

Actually thridging is one of the most pleasant and rewarding experiences in life. An uncle of mine thridged until the day of his death at 92. I myself will never forget thridging while drifting down the Rappahannock in a canoe in the cool of a summer evening. I thridged for seventeen miles. Some of the most famous names in history were ardent thridgers. Shakespeare never failed to thridge until dawn after every opening night. Cleopatra thridged infrequently but with a vigor that delighted her subjects. Stalin was a very poor thridger, Abraham Lincoln one of the best.

Many people contend that Watergate never would have happened if Haldeman, Ehrlichman and their cronies had devoted more time to thridging and less to hanging around microphones, yapping with the boss.

Thridge on, world!

Dr. David Viscott

    Dr. David Viscott stands at the forefront of one of the most important cultural phenomena of the late 20th century: the search for individual self-understanding. He has successfully taken his theories of psychiatry to the American masses through his best-selling books and popular radio and TV programs. He studied medicine at Tufts Medical School, and later turned to psychiatry as his specialty.

    In search for a location to begin practicing what is now considered his revolutionary short-term therapy method, he moved west and opened his acclaimed Viscott Center for Natural Therapy in Beverly Hills.

    His highly regarded books include How to Live With Another Person, Risking *and* Emotionally Free. *His latest book,* Finding Your Strength in Difficult Times, *is a volume of meditations and affirmations. He has recently completed* Toxic Nostalgia, *explaining the natural healing process.*

    Dr. Viscott has entered a new arena of the media with the completion of the filmscript of his popular book, The Making of a Psychiatrist.

Mesopotamia

My favorite word is **Mesopotamia**.

Some years ago when I was a student at Dartmouth I spoke with a young minister who had just started his pastoral service with a congregation across the Connecticut River in Vermont. He told the story of his first sermon. It was on a brilliant October Sunday, the foliage exploding, the scent of balsam enfranchising the fragrant air, the kind of day that reminds you of the divine presence itself. Eager to please he had spend weeks on that first sermon and delivered it with just enough seriousness to balance his youthful enthusiasm and convince his parishioners that they didn't make a mistake when they hired him.

After the sermon he went to the front door to greet his congregation and shake hands and, of course, to hear what he hoped would be lavish praise. Pride, he admitted, was still one of his failings.

"I so much loved your sermon this morning," an elderly woman effused.

"What part did you like?" the minister prompted, fully aware that he was in earshot of a dozen or so people still in line.

"Oh," the old woman cooed, still beaming with the transcendent rapture that had illuminated her being during the service. "I think it was when you mentioned that blessed name, Mesopotamia."

"The crowd started to giggle," the minister reported, still feeling embarrassed.

Since that conversation, Mesopotamia has become symbolic to me of the distance that stands between us, how we all live in our own worlds, how little we know what the other person is thinking and most importantly, how futile it is to try to please others.

Timothy Forbes

Son of the late multimillionaire Malcolm Forbes, Tim Forbes has made a name for himself as the president of the respected American Heritage *magazine. He follows a family tradition, since his grandfather founded* Forbes *magazine and his father, Malcolm Forbes, succeeded him as editor and publisher of* Forbes.

Under Malcolm Forbes' leadership, it became a highly successful publication. Tim Forbes has carried on the family tradition and has made American Heritage *a prestigious and profitable periodical with an expanding worldwide reputation.*

American

I like many words. "Absolutely," for example, punctuates my conversation when I'm happy or pleased. "Pretty" is a much-maligned word, often considered trivialization of "beauty" and still only skin deep. Yet for me, it is shorthand to express my deepest and most enduring feelings for my wife: "You're so pretty."

Still, the word I love, corny though it may seem, is **American**. It embraces so much and so many but is nonetheless specific. American describes a people, a place and a culture. It is an idea as well as an ideal, an identity and an identifiable style. You can eat it, wear it and play it. You can be it. You can also become it. The last is important. I fancy American equally for what it is not: a race, a social class, a religious creed, or a mere accident of geography, history or birth.

F. Scott Fitzgerald, in a very pretty phrase, called it "a willingness of the heart." Abraham Lincoln called it "the last best hope of earth." Absolutely.

Roger Staubach — Perseverance

Roger Staubach

This winner of both the 1963 Heisman and Maxwell Trophies graduated from the U.S. Naval Academy and fulfilled his military service in Vietnam prior to joining the Dallas Cowboys in 1969. He was the NFL's leading passer four times and quarterbacked his Cowboys to a equal number of conference championships. He was the team's leader in victories in Super Bowls VI and XII and was named Most Valuable Player in the 1972 game. Active in the Fellowship of Christian Athletes, Staubach's nickname was Captain Comeback, in recognition of his amazing ability to rally his teammates to victory in the closing minutes of crucial games.

Perseverance

When I add a new word to my vocabulary, I also try to incorporate its meaning in my lifestyle. And a word that I have been able to use actively is **perseverance**. I have included this word in my vocabulary because it indicates positive action. Its meaning is surrounded by strong words such as steadfastness and tenacity. To persevere is to set a goal, overcome the odds and achieve that goal. As Samuel Johnson said, "Great works are performed, not by strength, but perseverance."

My Word!

Lee Hills

From a news reporter in Price, Utah, to Chairman and Chief Executive Officer of Knight-Newspapers and Editorial Chief Emeritus of Knight-Ridder Newspapers, Lee Hills' domain included such diverse periodicals as the Akron Beacon Journal, *the* Columbus Enquirer, *the* Detroit Free Press, *the* Lexington Herald, *the* Tallahassee Democrat *the* Miami Herald *and the* Philadelphia Inquirer *and others.*

The leadership this native of Granville, North Dakota, demonstrated in his lengthy career as a reporter, editor and publisher resulted in a Pulitzer Prize in 1956 and the presidency of Sigma Delta Chi, the professional journalism fraternity.

The dictionary

We have been going through a period when the spoken use of the language, especially among the young, has deteriorated. A jerky, mumbling incoherence seems to substitute for clear thought and precise expression for many, because for them that is the chic way to talk.

I do believe that young people will begin to shake off their obsession with conformity, will reverse this putdown of the language and the widespread use of four-letter and other "dirty words" to express everything—and nothing.

The creative use of words, developed and refined over the centuries, is one of the crowning achievements of civilization, and it is encouraging to me to see that it is no longer such an "in" thing to be inarticulate.

The English language, particularly, is precise beyond all others and has great range and power to articulate the human condition.

For a word, I give you **the dictionary**!

Ralph de Toledano

Ralph de Toledano was born in the International Zone of Tangier. He built a solid reputation as an incisive columnist, author and lecturer. A former assistant editor of Newsweek, *he served as Washington correspondent for the King Features Syndicate and Copley News Service. He was contributing editor for the* National Review *and was the recipient of three Freedoms Foundation Awards for his writings.*

His books include Seeds of Treason, *the story of the Alger Hiss case;* Spies, Dupes and Diplomats; Hit and Run: the Rise—and Fall?—of Ralph Nader *and biographies of Richard Nixon, Robert F. Kennedy and J. Edgar Hoover.*

De Toledano's lifelong love of language and the derivation of words is reflected in the selection of his favorites.

MY WORD!

I love them all

What is my favorite word? How can I tell? As a child, I roamed the dictionaries—English, French, Spanish—looking for words that had an interesting sound or pattern of letters, an intriguing meaning. I loved "tintinnabulation" for its onomatopoeia, "concatenation" for its concept of linkage. I was delighted by "adamantine" when I came across it in *Paradise Lost*.

But the words I enjoyed most were those with a story behind them. Take cavalier, for example, derived from the French *chevalier,* the Spanish *caballero* and the Italian *cavaliere.* Why should a horseman or a knight derive from the Latin caballus, a nag or worthless horse, instead of equus? An etymologist gave me the answer. Roman officers used to refer affectionately to their horses as nags or old nags. As Latin slipped into the vulgar tongues, the spoken speech was what made the greatest imprint.

Or place names. I am always amused when Mexicans sing romantic songs about Guadalajara. They took the name from a river in Spain, a muddy river which the Arabs called the *guad el khra*, the river of excrement.

I ask myself why two words coming from the same root, the Latin *plangore* should have much different meanings: plangent, meaning noisy, as the clash of many bells; and plangorous, meaning wailing or full of lamentation.

What is my favorite word? **I love them all**.

Bart Starr

At one time, Bart Starr was listed by the United States Postal Service as one of the nation's ten top recipients of mail. His popularity was a result of exploits such as those taking place in 19-below weather in Green Bay in 1967 in an NFL championship game known today as the Ice Bowl. With just 16 seconds to play, quarterback Bart Starr's unforgettable 1-yard touchdown sneak won that memorable game 21-17 for coach Vince Lombardi.

Following his distinguished career as quarterback with the Green Bay Packers, after being named Most Valuable Player in Super Bowls I and II, he joined his former NFL teammates as their coach. His honors include being selected Player of the Decade in 1970 and being inducted into professional football's Hall of Fame seven years later. Starr became a successful entrepreneur in a number of business ventures. In recent years, he has been active in helping young people as well as adults work together toward a Drug Free America.

His advice has the ring of one who practices what he preaches.

Attitude

There are many words which have a special meaning to all of us, but perhaps the one which means more to me is **attitude**.

Having been privileged to be associated with many fine people during my football career, I found that there was a key or secret ingredient, if you will, in their success. . .a winning attitude.

Attitude is not something you are born with, it is a part of our lives over which each man has control. The person who approaches life with a positive attitude, a player who enters the contest with a winning attitude, will emerge victorious.

Attitude, quite simply, is the difference between being just a participant or being a champion.

Santa Claus

Santa Claus

Photo by Dr. Leo Cummins

Perhaps it's his flowing white hair and beard, his twinkly eyes and impish smile. Or maybe it's his love of children of all ages—or the way he fits so well into that red velvet suit with the rabbit fur trim. Whatever the reason, author Vick Knight is asked to portray Santa Claus dozens of times each December. Here, he offers a favorite word that occurs to him every year in the persona of Old St. Nick.

MY WORD!

Giving

As I put on my red suit and tassled cap and pull on my shiny boots and white gloves each Christmas season, one word comes to mind. That word is **giving**. Oh, I'm not talking about brightly wrapped packages with big bows or even the candy canes I carry with me to hand out. From the tiniest toddler at the nursery schools to the most senior citizen in the rest homes, I am aware of the gift of giving—giving that really counts.

Children and adults alike give me a brilliant smile, and often a hug, when I walk in the door. Well-dressed men and women pulling up beside me in their expensive vehicles give me a wave. Teenage boys and girls, who are supposed to be too mature to believe in me anymore, give me "high fives" or pats on the back. People from all walks of life go out of their way to give me a friendly word.

Wouldn't it be wonderful if we could all be more giving this way all year round? Why not try it? Give someone a smile, a kind word, a friendly wave.

It might make their day—and yours.

Milton Caniff

Milton Caniff

Milton Caniff began his career as a cartoonist at the age of fourteen in Dayton, Ohio. As the creator of such popular series as "Dickie Dare," "Terry and the Pirates," "Male Call," and "Steve Canyon," his lengthy career made him among the best known and recognized of comic strip artists. His drawings won him the George Washington Honor Medal of the Freedoms Foundation at Valley Forge, the Medal of Merit Award from the United States Air Force Association and the Goodwill Industries Award for his original design of the character Good Willie.

His work with action-adventure newspaper comic strip heroes was greatly admired for its realistic detail in the drawings and story line since mood, atmosphere and evocation were the trademarks of his work. In 1995 the United States Postal Service honored him and his "Terry and the Pirates" comic strip in a special series of commemorative postage stamps, one of which is pictured here.

MY WORD!

Meanwhile

Meanwhile is more than a word! It is a crutch, a tool, a cop-out, a salvation for the continuity cartoon writer and artist on such strips as "Steve Canyon."

When we have characters in a mass of travail to which no solution seems possible, we haul out the trusty doorstop of "meanwhile, back at the ranch" (or base, or ground control, or you name it). It is like an orchestra vamping until the singer can remember the words to the song.

The mother lode for this endless treasure is the virtuoso performance of Scheherazade, when she conned the sultan into delaying her execution at each suceeding dawn—until, after 1001 Arabian Nights, he finally put her on the full-tme payroll (probably so he could get some sleep).

I suspect that the bright babe's full married name was Mrs. Scheherazade Meanwhile Shahrisar.*

*Of course you know that was the old boy's name.

Walter Knott

Photo by Gittings

Long before ground was broken for Disneyland in California's Orange County, Walter Knott had a well-established tourist attraction in Buena Park. Starting with a small roadside stand offering berries and pies for sale, Knott's Berry Farm is now a major player in the billion-dollar Southern California amusement park scene. With major rides and attractions, this sprawling site has become a vacation destination for both international and domestic travelers. Knott himself was well known for his conservative beliefs and support of political figures that met his qualifications for leadership. His family assumed management of Knott's Berry Farm following his death.

Perseverance

Everyone needs a goal in life to achieve anything worthwhile.

If we do not have a goal, how will we know when we have arrived?

The experience of a long life has taught me that a goal must be linked to **perseverance**, in order to have a satisfying and successful life. This is why perseverance is an important word to me. In fact, perseverance can be more important than brilliance or skill. Even hard work can become mere drudgery to the person who does not persevere toward some goal.

This word perseverance has the basic meaning of being set, or fixed. So when problems arise or opposition comes, the one who has perseverance will not give way or give up. I am grateful that the Knott family has had a goal, and the perseverance needed to keep heading in the direction of that goal. Without this combination, Knott's Berry Farm would never have grown to the point where we employ thousands of people and can provide good entertainment and quality products for several million visitors each year.

Vin Scully

 The Voice of the Los Angeles Dodgers may have had the most recognizable style of delivery of any major league baseball announcer. His career at the microphone outlasted most of the athletes whose accomplishments and failures he documented on radio and television. He began his broadcasting career at Fordham University, in New York, announcing baseball, basketball and football games over the school's radio station.

 Just a year after his graduation, he joined the Brooklyn Dodger broadcasting team, merging with Hall of Fame announcers Red Barber and Connie Desmond. A master of the English language, this favorite of Dodger fans was voted the Most Memorable Personality in Los Angeles Dodger history. From New York to L.A. and everywhere between, Scully has covered many of baseball's thrilling games, moments and achievements.

 In addition to his work on Dodger baseball, Scully announces the World Series on the CBS Radio Network. He's broadcast a dozen World Series and six All-Star Games for television. He's been honored by his peers as Outstanding Sportscaster in the Nation four times and was inducted into the American Sportscasters Hall of Fame in 1992.

Home

For the past 47 years I have been careening across the country in the company of the Brooklyn and now Los Angeles Dodgers.

I have ridden upper berths, lower berths, roomettes and bedrooms, dozed fitfully against the cold leather of a Greyhound bus and sat red eyed and restless in countless hotel lobbies, train stations and airports.

I have flown everything from an antiquated DC3 to the incredible 747 and have dined on everything from tacos in Mexico City to tempura in Tokyo.

I have lugged attaché cases, briefcases, suitcases and trunks not to mention the ever-present carryall. I have covered a couple of million miles and used enough words to at least rival the national debt.

My favorite word is the most important word in baseball. It is the beginning and the end of every game and the start and finish of every road trip . . . the word is **home**.

George Gallup, Jr.

George Gallup, Jr., chairman of the George H. Gallup International Institute, has followed his family's tradition of conducting public opinion polls on social and economic issues and current events. The Gallup Poll pioneered scientifically based surveys using samples of representative populations. Through the sales of the results of these polls to the media and other interested individuals, the institute finances its studies.

Forgiveness

My favorite word is **forgiveness**—a gentle sounding word, but a concept of great power: to forgive is to be strong, not weak.

Forgiveness is part of the proverbial wisdom that is embedded in our Judeo Christian culture. It seems that in today's world we need to re-examine the concept of forgiveness, and to remind ourselves of its miraculous power to heal broken relationships in our hurting and fragmented society when nothing else seems to work. Forgiveness taps the best that is in the human spirit and is, I believe, God-given. Most Americans would agree: three in four believe that one must rely on God's help to truly forgive someone from the heart.

Harry Golden

As editor of The Carolina Israelite, *Harry Golden was responsible for what was known as The Most Widely Quoted Personal Journal in the World. A prolific author, his books included* Only in America; For 2c Plain; Enjoy, Enjoy; So Long as You're Healthy; The Golden Book of Jewish Humor; The Greatest Jewish City in the World *and* The Autobiography of Harry Golden.

Lazy words

I like lazy words.

The English language has several dozen ugly words, like "dichotomy" and "bifurcation," about which we can do nothing since they already mean (I believe the professional semanticists say "signify" or "connote") something. We certainly make no improvement when we infest the language with our lazy words—words like "gimmick," which does not even mean, connote or signify much of anything at all. "Give me the picture," the boss says to the salesman. Just what in hell does the boss want?

Even worse is the word "thing." "Thing" means or fails to mean a million situations. The financial report becomes "the whole thing."

"The thing is getting out of hand," says the boss to his secretary, meaning his wife has found out about their casual evenings together.

"Get your things on," says the mother to her children. She wants them to dress.

"A funny thing happened to me . . . ."

Joan Dial

Joan Dial

Joan Dial also writes as Katherine Sinclair, Amanda York, Katherine Kent and Paige Phillips. She's the author of 25 novels (family sagas, mysteries, historical romances, contemporary women's fiction) published in the United States and 30 foreign countries. She has also published a number of non-fiction pieces, including "how-to" articles, and has lectured extensively on the subject of creative writing.

Some of her titles include Through the Years, Dare to Dream, From a Far Country, Roses in Winter *and* Echoes of War.

Born in Liverpool, England, Joan married an American and then, in her words, "proceeded to fall in love with his country and live happily ever after." Parents of two sons and a daughter, the Dials currently live in Southern California.

Harmony

I am delighted to contribute my word for inclusion.

Harmony . . . because it signifies that elusive state of being we all crave.

We hear a coincident combination of musical tones by merely murmuring the word, and we think of friendship, of a fitting together, of accord, inner calm, a pleasing integration of components.

Family harmony, global harmony, singing in harmony, harmony of color, texture, the harmony of nature.

As a writer occupying five personae, each writing fiction, and since basically, all fiction is actually friction, harmony is of necessity lacking in my professional life, but wonderfully present in my personal life.

Harmony is what I wish for everyone, everywhere.

Ann Landers

Born as Esther Pauline Friedman in Sioux City, Iowa, this prolific journalist has developed an international following after taking over a Chicago newspaper column titled "Ann Landers." She has continued as a major syndicated figure along with her twin sister, Abigail Van Buren. Her advice on myriad topics has resulted in numerous public service awards and recognition as a positive influence on American life. Her books include The Ann Landers Encyclopedia *and* Ann Landers Talks to Teen-Agers About Sex.

Try

My favorite word is **try**.

No one knows the extent of his capabilities unless he meets the challenge, makes the effort and tries.

Too many people don't try because they are afraid of failure. How they cheat themselves! It saddens me to think of the things undone that need doing—the zillions of opportunities passed up because someone was afraid to try.

I would much rather try and fail fifty times than not try and never know whether or not I could have made it.

Mario Pei

Among the premier names in American philology, is Mario Andrew Pei. His books include A Diet of Linguistics *and* The Family of Words. *From his Glen Ridge, New Jersey, office he offers the following lesson.*

A word lesson

English is a language that lends itself to confusion and contradiction.

Examples of the first are the common confusion between principal and principle, and between its and it's. Principal is both noun and adjective (the principal of a school, the principal and the interest, as against the principal cause of the error); principle is only a noun (first principles of mathematics, a man of principle). It's is an abbreviated form of it is, and the apostrophe marks the elision of the second "i"; its is the possessive form of it, and means "belonging to it."

Typical of confusions that appear in speech as well as in writing are the use of infer for imply, and of bi-monthly for semi-monthly. Infer means to deduce or understand on the basis of available evidence (from the man's speech, he inferred that he was a foreigner); imply is to hint, to convey information in a roundabout manner (he didn't specifically say so, but he implied to me that the man was a foreigner). The bi- of bi-monthly could mean twice a month but also every two months; the semi- of semi-monthly means half (every half month). Obviously, it is bi- that is confusing (note that biannual means twice a year, biennial every two years) ; but semi- has only one meaning, and is crystal clear. It might be suggested that bi- be restricted to the meaning of "every two." Unfortunately, the English language goes not by logic, but by usage, and logical reforms do not find ready acceptance.

Lucille Ball

A native of Jamestown, New York, Lucille Ball was fifteen years old when she went to New York City to study drama under the celebrated John Murray Anderson. Between acting in small parts on the stage, she supported herself by taking jobs as a secretary, waitress and model. She launched her motion picture career in 1933 as an extra and later appeared as a Goldwyn Girl in a film featuring Eddie Cantor. It wasn't long before she had established herself as film's leading female clown, co-starring with such counterparts as Red Skelton and Bob Hope.

In 1940, she met and later married Desi Arnaz, a Cuban bandleader, and they collaborated in the 1950s in developing and co-starring in television's prototypical situation comedy, "I Love Lucy." They founded Desilu Productions and became successful producers of television shows while pioneering innovative approaches to filming techniques.

After their divorce in 1960, Miss Ball became the CEO of Desilu, a CEO of a corporation annually grossing more that twenty-five million dollars. She was honored by both the public and the entertainment industry as a certified Superstar. Her lengthy and prolific life's work provided laughter and escape to three generations of loyal fans. Mame was the final motion picture in her illustrious career.

Beauty

Choosing a favorite word reminds me of the little boy in the candy store. He likes all the goodies, but can buy only one. Two minutes after he buys the sucker, he wishes he'd bought the peppermint stick.

That's the way I feel about words. I love them all, but to pick one favorite leaves out a lot of goodies. So, with some reservation, if I had to make a choice, I suppose the word would be **beauty**. Not in the common connotation, but for what it implies in a spiritual and moral sense.

You can find beauty everywhere—in people, places, things and thoughts. Beauty is rampant in nature—from a snow-covered mountain to a lone blossom in the desert. You can find beauty in people—how they live, think and work.

There is beauty in a home, not necessarily because of its decor, but for the atmosphere created by its dwellers. Then, of course, there is the spiritual beauty that so many people possess, which helps them and others to live a beautiful life.

As Keats expressed it, "A thing of beauty is a joy forever."

Pat Boone

Pat Boone has gone about as far as one can go from Nashville, Tennessee, where he grew up, was class president, newspaper editor and captain of the baseball team at Lipscomb High School. He had hoped to teach high school himself in those days — even started college in Texas and received a magna cum laude *degree from Columbia University. But a career in the entertainment world intervened, and resulted in international acclaim for Boone as an actor, author, recording artist, radio and TV personality, sportsman and religious leader.*

His recording of "Love Letters in the Sand" remained on the best-selling charts for 34 consecutive weeks, and this and his other songs sold more than 4.5 million records. His 1995 anniversary tour came on the heels of his portrayal of Will Rogers in the musical comedy, The Will Rogers Follies.

Pat and his wife, Shirley, have four daughters and fifteen grandchildren and continue to be active church members. He is the recipient of the Israeli government's Israel Cultural Award and has been named by the Israeli Tourism Department as Christian Ambassador to Israel.

Daddy

I still call my father Daddy.

My four daughters call me Daddy, too. My grandchildren, 15 in number, all call me Daddy Pat.

I love the word **Daddy**.

In a society where family relationships are struggling, where the institution of family itself is under multiple attack, where it is projected that fifty percent of our children—or more—born around the turn of this new century will be raised in single parent families, the word Daddy takes on enormous new significance.

God likes the word Daddy too, though in the Bible, and in Hebrew, the word is Abba. In the eighth chapter of Romans, and in other places as well, God said He actually wants us to know Him not just as Father, but even more intimately as Daddy or Abba. How fantastic! Every association and connotation of the word Daddy is good—parental care and support, fun and fellowship, wise advice and stirring example. God wants us to know, "I'll be that for you. I want to be your Daddy."

I can't imagine anything better.

Rev. Billy Graham

William Franklin "Billy" Graham is perhaps the world's leading evangelist. A native of South Carolina, he continues to maintain the headquarters for his international ministry in Montreat, North Carolina. Dr. Graham's Christian Crusades have taken him to practically every country and, until recently, he still found the time to write a daily newspaper column dealing with the spiritual needs of millions of readers. He is the founder of World Wide Pictures, Inc., and for years was featured on the "Hour of Decision" radio and television series.

Decision

People come up to me and say, "Why should I make a **decision** about God? I'm happy doing what I'm doing. You call it sin, I call it fun. Live and let live."

If they don't say it in these words, the thought's there unspoken, in their faces. There's pleasure in sin — but only for a season. Deep down there is a gnawing, dull dissatisfaction.

I sat down with a 69-year-old business executive in a large eastern city recently who told me, "I have fifty million dollars and everything I could ever want—and I am the most miserable man in this city."

One of the biggest names in Hollywood, a tall, strapping, swash-buckling type, revealed the same thing in different words. His life, he admitted, was lonely and empty.

These two prominent people have discovered that wealth and fame aren't enough in life. Millions more feel the same way. Telling lies and dodging the facts cannot shield them from the real truth —that because their consciences are black with acts against God, they can find no inner peace. To cleanse out this dirt, they need the injection of a driving spiritual force in their lives.

Jim Vaus came out of World War II a master of electronics. Within a few years he was in the employ of big gamblers on the

Rev. Billy Graham (continued)

West Coast, drawing down huge fees for his craftsmanship at wire tapping and communications.

One night Jim dropped in on one of our meetings in Los Angeles to kill time before he was to take off by plane for a very important deal in St. Louis. Outwardly indifferent, he stood at the rear of the hall. When the call came for those in the audience to come forward and made a decision for Christ, a quiet man next to big Jim tapped him on the shoulder.

"Will you go forward with me?"

Jim whirled on him. "Lay off me or I'll knock your head off."

The other man didn't retreat. "You can do anything you like to me," he said gently, "but that won't right things between you and God."

Something clicked inside of Jim Vaus at that moment. His face twisted with emotion, he started walking to the front of the hall. Jim then made a decision to break clean with his old life and contacts. Today, he is one of the Lord's hardest workers.

Jim Vaus found out later that the plane he didn't catch that night of decision was met in St. Louis by gunmen who had instructions to kill him.

This is a spectacular example of what God can do with a person.

Billy Graham's "Decision" essay printed with permission from Guideposts Magazine. Copyright © 1951 by Guideposts, Carmel, New York, 10512.

MY WORD!

Joan Embery

Photo by R. Garrison, San Diego Zoo

Whether appearing with Johnny Carson on "The Tonight Show" with some of her exotic animals or providing close-up and hands-on demonstrations at the famed San Diego Zoo, Joan Embery has been a most effective goodwill ambassador for wildlife during her tenure with that popular park. Her ability to capture the attention of TV viewers with a seemingly endless parade of furry, scaled and feathered creatures has been an effective component of her life's work, combining education and entertainment.

She's pictured here as she celebrated her twenty-fifth year with the zoo. Embery has devoted her career to teaching people, young and old, about wildlife and conservation through her numerous national and local television appearances and speeches.

Animals

Animals.

I can't imagine a world without them. Beauty, strength, survival, adaptability and uniqueness are all qualities represented in our diverse animal world.

William Anders

Apollo-Saturn 8 astronaut William Anders has led a vigorous life since the first lunar orbit and lunar return re-entry, when views of the moon's surface were televised back to earth. He continued to serve his country in such capacities as Executive Secretary of the National Aeronautics and Space Council, Chairman of the Nuclear Regulatory Commission and United States Ambassador to Norway. His contribution to this book may, in some small way, allude to the fact that his space travel was in a craft constructed by the low bidder.

Explore

My favorite word is **explore**. I use it in many ways, but mostly when I mean "to learn more about something." There is an old expression that I like which I try to emulate. It has to do with doing things well. It defines a "master craftsman."

A worker works with his hands.
A craftsman works with his hands and his mind.
But a master craftsman works with his hands,
his mind and his heart.

David Wolper

David L. Wolper earned fame as a TV and motion picture producer. Following early success in documentaries, he moved on to full-length feature films including Willie Wonka and the Chocolate Factory *and* Visions of Eight. *When tapped by Peter Ueberroth to oversee the various productions for the 1984 Los Angeles Olympic Games, his theatrical and planning talents resulted in one of the most successful and self-supporting games in history.*

Planning

If I have to choose one word—that word would be **planning**. Everything I do, whether going on a holiday, going out for an evening, or figuring my work for the future, always involves planning. It is one of the keys to success, both in business and personal life.

Planning something before you do it assures you that, when it happens, it will not only be good but, because of your planning, it will indeed happen. Planning means knowing where you are going and that you're going to get there. It is a word and action that has been the keystone of my whole life.

Herman Wouk

Herman Wouk first gained literary prominence as a comedy writer for the Fred Allen radio series. His subsequent service in the United States Navy provided a wealth of background material for his future volumes. Wouk's serious works elevated him to a place of honor among major international contemporary writers, as well as a Pulitzer Prize for The Caine Mutiny in 1952. Marjorie Morningstar, Youngblood Hawke, Aurora Dawn, The Hope, The Glory and The Winds of War are among his best-known novels. The latter was produced as a TV mini-series and achieved great success.

Wouk's long-awaited sequel to The Winds of War titled War and Remembrance, won critical acclaim as a novel and a popular TV movie.

No

On my desk a hand-printed motto reads, "The most important word in your vocabulary is **no**."

That has a heartless, not to say icy, sound to it. The intent is quite the opposite.

Once a man passes thirty, many interests beckon to him; many responsibilities pluck at him. This is as true in art as in worldly affairs.

Creative visions crowd on most writers, composers, and painters; but art is long, time is short, and to attempt all is to fail all.

To do a few things well, one must cut off many things. It is the principle of pruning. Giving of yourself is happiness; squandering yourself is misery.

The dividing line between the two is no.

Glen Campbell

Photo by Sandra Gillard

As the Rhinestone Cowboy who made such songs as "The Wichita Lineman" and "Galveston" popular hits, Glen Campbell continues to please concert crowds from stages throughout the country. He was the recipient of the Grammy Award from the National Academy of Recording Arts & Sciences in 1968 for his popular album, "By the Time I Get to Phoenix." His honors include recognition as America's Entertainer of the Year, the TV Personality of the Year, and countless other awards. It was a long trip from Delight, Arkansas, to musical stardom, but Glen Campbell has carried off this excursion in great style. He's a singer, songwriter, movie actor and golfer . . . and says he takes the time to enjoy his good fortune with perception and gratitude.

Appreciate

I fell into a habit a few years back. I got to saying, "I **appreciate** it."

It generally followed thank you, and it has become a personal kind of emphasis to the point that, yes, I really am thankful. It has become kind of a trademark, too, but I don't mind.

There's so much going on for everyone to appreciate nowadays, and there's nothing wrong with sharing a positive, progressive kind of feeling. I enjoy letting people know that, for every person spreading gloom, there's somebody else spreading the good times.

Getting invited to pick a word or so, getting myself into a book with such good company, is one of those times, so thank you. I appreciate it.

Christine Todd Whitman

The Honorable Christine Todd Whitman was elected the fiftieth governor of the state of New Jersey in 1993, and became the first woman in the state's history to win its highest elective office.

During her years in public life, Governor Whitman has served on a variety of boards, commissions and other volunteer bodies. She carries on a long tradition of public service. Her parents, the late Eleanor and Webster Todd, served the Republican Party and their state and country in numerous positions, which ranged from vice chairman of the Republican National Committee to State GOP Chairman. In addition to her public service, she has devoted much of her life to raising a family. Her husband, John R. Whitman, is a financial consultant with political roots of his own—his grandfather was governor of New York, and his father was a circuit judge. The Whitmans have two teenage children.

MY WORD!

Clearly

In response to your request for my choice of a favorite word, I submit one that not only conveys an essential aspect of my philosophy on communication but also serves as a valuable tool. That word is **clearly**.

Communication of any kind, whether it be a late-night conversation with a daughter, a carefully worded letter to a political adversary, or an enthusiastic address to an enthusiastic audience, fails without clarity. Wasted words equal wasted time, and no one makes progress toward any end without crafting his or her message with care. Being heard is nothing without being understood.

As a tool for use in communicating concisely, the word provides simple but effective emphasis for any statement of truth: "Clearly, New Jersey is a great state"; or "Clearly, the Garden State boasts a talented and diverse population, tremendous natural beauty, and wonderful opportunities for businesses of every type and size." Clearly, I love New Jersey, and will take advantage of every chance I get to say so.

I hope I've made myself clearly understood.

Col. Harland Sanders

Harland Sanders, with a sixth grade education, began twenty-five years of odd jobs including service in the U.S. Army in Cuba. In 1929, this native of Henryville, Indiana, opened a combination gas station/small restaurant in Corbin, Kentucky, and later came up with a procedure of using a pressure cooker to prepare chicken quickly. After World War II, a new interstate by-passed his restaurant and he was forced to sell his place of business. He took to the road, demonstrating his cooking technique and "secret blend of herbs and spices" to other restaurateurs, and this led to the sale in 1956 of five franchises. Four years later, he had sold two hundred, and this was only the start of the Colonel Sanders phenomenon. The designation of Colonel was not for military service; rather, it was conferred by the Governor of Kentucky in recognition of the entrepreneur's culinary contributions.

Sanders received the prestigious Horatio Alger Award before he died in 1980. His likeness, such as the one painted by Norman Rockwell and printed here, is featured throughout the world at thousands of restaurants where Kentucky Fried Chicken is sold.

Integrity

Integrity. That's the word. It's the most important word I can think of. My mother taught me the meaning of the word when I was very young. And I've built my life on it.

Integrity means being true, dependable and honest. When you're working for a man, it means delivering your best effort. When you're an employer, it means treating your co-workers fairly. In business, it means providing the customer with an honest product at reasonable cost.

Integrity is a better guarantee than all the legal contracts ever written. Integrity is more than truth. It's truth backed by determined honesty and a fundamental morality.

Dr. Joyce Brothers

Dr. Joyce Brothers

Psychologist, television celebrity and internationally syndicated radio personality, Dr. Joyce Brothers first won fame as a successful contestant with an amazing knowledge of boxing on "The $64,000 Question" and the "$64,000 Challenge" quiz shows. She is said to have memorized volumes of boxing information prior to her appearances. Those feats earned her tremendous publicity as both a female and an intellectual who was an expert on the manly art of self defense!

She earned her Ph.D. in psychology from Columbia University, and following her radio fame, began a lengthy media career on her own "Dr. Joyce Brothers" series. Television appearances and her syndicated newspaper columns soon followed. She has continued to be among the most popular of no-nonsense media psychological counselors.

Her ten books have been translated into twenty-six languages. They include How to Get Whatever You Want Out of Life *and* What Every Woman Should Know About Men.

My Word!

Tenderness

A funny thing happened on our way to the sexual revolution. We misplaced **tenderness**. Worse, we placed a taboo on it. "Sex is an instinct that must not be repressed!" seems to be our call to arms. The arms too often offer physical closeness while denying emotional involvement. Can man live on physical love alone? Not very fully, I'm afraid.

Tenderness is one of the infant's first and strongest needs. Thrust from the warm womb into the cold world, he associates this need with hunger and its gratification with being fed. The mother gives him his first lesson in love with warm milk. She cuddles and coos, snuggles and rocks, and wraps the child in physical warmth and total caring. Babies in institutions who don't get this tender, loving care don't thrive as well as babies who do. Its effect can be measured in inches of growth and in pounds of weight gain.

But too soon and totally the taboo against tenderness takes over. Mama is so afraid her little boy won't turn into a great big he-man that she refuses to let him learn the lessons of independence gradually, the way he learned to walk and to talk. Once

Dr. Joyce Brothers (continued)

thrust out of Mama's lap, the expulsion is forever. The child is called a baby if he wants to return and ridiculed as a sissy if he tries to regain the tenderness he has lost when he cuddles playmates, pets or toys. In this way he learns to deny his own need for emotional love at the same time that he is denied the opportunity to learn how to express the tenderness he may feel for others.

As he matures, his parents, and even the schools, may teach him about physical love as if there were no other kind. This knowledge is supposed to remove the inhibitions from which his Victorian ancestors suffered and make him healthy and happy. But does it? Not always. The grown-up for whom physical passion is not enough may try to regain the larger love he knew as an infant, and which he still associates with hunger and its satisfaction. To you he may look like a drunkard, a glutton or a drug addict. Only his psychiatrist knows that he's really a man searching desperately for tenderness.

Lowell Thomas

Lowell Thomas traveled a long way from his home in Cripple Creek, Colorado, to Samarkand in his career of forty-six years as a broadcaster. He retired in 1976 so that he might devote additional time to his many interests. During his lengthy and colorful life's work, he worked as a reporter, teacher, author, lecturer, and media personality. From 1930 to 1976, he traveled to exotic places throughout the world, narrated weekly Movietone newsreels and travelogues for Twentieth Century Fox, and was the author of a number of popular books. He broadcast from numerous scenes of combat during World War II and later profiled many outstanding historical personalities on the Public Broadcasting System. He often modestly claimed that his fame on radio was due to the fact that his show originally preceded the enormously popular "Amos 'n' Andy."

His enthusiasm for such diverse projects as the exploits of Lawrence of Arabia to the experimentation leading to the development of Cinerama leads one to believe that he did not select his word in a cursory manner.

Enthusiasm

Alas, I haven't any one word in mind. But, if you must have one, how about the word **enthusiasm**? If you have enthusiasm, usually nearly everything else falls into place sooner or later.

President Gerald Ford

The thirty-eighth President of the United States, this Omaha, Nebraska, native is a graduate of the University of Michigan and Yale Law School. He enlisted in the U.S. Navy during World War II and was selected to his first term in the House of Representatives in 1949. He was elected by his peers to serve as House Minority Leader in 1965 and, on the resignation of Spiro T. Agnew in 1973, was named by President Richard Nixon to assume the position of Vice-President. When Nixon resigned under pressure in 1974, Gerald Rudolph Ford, Jr. became the President. He lost the 1976 presidential election to Jimmy Carter and then retired from an active role in politics. He currently resides in Rancho Mirage, California.

MY WORD!

Affirmative

I am by nature an optimist. I never see the glass as half empty but as half full. I stress the **affirmative**, never the negative, and so the word affirmative is a favorite with me. My outlook is much like that of Dr. Norman Vincent Peale in his book, *The Power of Positive Thinking*. My philosophy is that human beings destroy themselves by emphasizing the negative. Their approach should always be affirmative. I call this the "I think I can" philosophy. If you think you can, then you can and you will. This is the basic ingredient of success, the absolute essential for progress. The word affirmative has become associated in my mind with positive action, with achievement, with getting things done. With affirmative action comes the solid sense of satisfaction derived from accomplishing a difficult or seemingly impossible task.

And, of course, for any man in political life, an affirmative vote is necessary from the people he represents if he is to continue in the profession of politics. So from my point of view, the word affirmative signifies a continuation of a way of life I enjoy and, even more importantly it signifies that the people for whom I speak feel some measure of confidence and trust in me.

Larry Speakes

Larry M. Speakes majored in journalism at the University of Mississippi and began his communications career as a newspaper editor. He went to Washington in 1968 as Press Secretary to the late Senator James O. Eastland and moved to the White House in 1974, serving the terms of Richard M. Nixon and Gerald R. Ford. Speakes was Chief Spokesperson for the President during the administration of Ronald Reagan. In 1987, Reagan awarded him the Presidential Citizen's Medal, the nation's second-highest civilian award.

Speakes currently is the Senior Vice President for Corporate and Legislative Affairs for the United States Postal Service.

Family

I have given great thought to the selection of a favorite word. Many, of course, come to mind. Words such as history, change, accountability and action are among those I considered. But when all is said and done, I believe the word that matters most to me is **family**.

There is no way to adequately express how much my own family—my parents, my wife, my three children and my two grandchildren—mean to me. They have always been the center of my life, whether at a moment of great achievement or disappointment, and everything in between.

Many people in public life are talking about family values these days. Well, for me, it might make sense to reverse that to values family. I always have, and for what it's worth, I think if more people did, they would find their lives happier.

Walter Brennan

Walter Brennan was the first actor to win three Academy Awards for best supporting actor. He received this recognition for his memorable appearances in Come and Get It, Kentucky and The Westerner. This Massachusetts native appeared in more than a hundred films during his distinguished motion picture career and was honored by his election to Oklahoma's National Cowboy Hall of Fame. Brennan also received the coveted George Washington Medal of Freedom from the Freedoms Foundation at Valley Forge.

He was trained in engineering, but instead entered the acting profession and appeared with several stock companies and in vaudeville, meanwhile supporting himself as a bank clerk and lumberjack. He made his initial impact in Hollywood as a stuntman and extra in 1923, and later became one of the best-known and most versatile supporting players in an amazing scope of character roles.

He died at eighty years of age, a keen and dedicated student of America's history and heritage.

MY WORD!

Separate

The entertainment industry strives not for vocabulary, but for an absence of it. The primary objective is to be understood. Dialogue, therefore, does not usually seek to educate but rather to communicate, and to do so with clarity not cluttered up with intellectual buttons and bows. Some critics regard this as an indictment of the media. In any case, it is a fact of life to the performer.

Of course, what an actor does on his own time is his own business. I like to read. And I have many favorite words, cherished for their delicate nuances and, in some instances, their ancestry. Caprice, for example, with its derivation from a "goat's head." Or pumpernickel, which you may wish to check out with Mr. Webster before using again. But the word most likely to light up my face when I hear it, or read it, is a simple one. I refer to the verb **separate**. I would like to share with you the reasons for giving it special significance.

I was a third grade student at the old Robinson Street School in Lynn, Massachusetts, and my grade in spelling would have been perfect except for one mistake. I substituted an "e" in place of an "a" in the second syllable of the word "separate." The word came out "seperate."

Inasmuch as this is a frequent error, even among adults, I do

Walter Brennan (continued)

not associate my failure with any traumatic experience. What I recall so vividly is what my teacher, Miss Lamont, said when she corrected me. First, she wrote the word correctly on the blackboard. Then she erased the two letters, "p" and "a," and asked me to name them. I did.

"Now, Walter," she asked, "what do those two letters spell, all by themselves?"

"Pa," I replied.

"Exactly," she said. "Now look at the word again, Walter, and try always to remember: If you take away the 'Pa,' you separate the family.

I never again forgot how to spell that word. More important, perhaps, I never forgot that Miss Lamont was teaching all of us two things at once. Besides correcting my spelling error, she was impressing our class with the value of the family as a unit.

Particularly in this day of global thinking, when the family as a cohesive force appears to be lost in the meat-grinder of computer humanity, I often think of that word and how it came to have a very special meaning to me.

Dan Jansen ══════════════════════ Effort

Dan Jansen

Speedskater Dan Jansen's repeated bad luck included failing in his specialty races in both the 1988 Calgary and the 1992 Albertville Olympic Games. In spite of his world records set in non-Olympic races, the Gold Medal eluded him. It appeared that the 1994 Games in Lillehammer would also deny him that goal when he lost his balance in the 500 meter finals and finished eighth. His last chance to redeem himself came in the 1000 meter finals. Again, he briefly lost his balance but, with great determination and fortitude, he regained his momentum and brought his American teammates the gold medal he had sought so long.

Effort

I think my favorite word is **effort**. After everything I have been through in my athletic career, I have truly come to appreciate effort. It may be a cliché, but I firmly believe that the victory comes in the struggle and the effort to be the best you can be at whatever you choose to do in life. I see too many people who are so naturally gifted that they don't have to work very hard to keep up, but they never see their full potential because they never give one hundred percent effort. Be the best you can be!

═══════════════════════════ My Word!

Joan Crawford — Time

Joan Crawford

Born in San Antonio, Texas, as Lucille Fay Le Sueur, this acclaimed film actress distinguished herself in perhaps the widest spectrum of roles in the annals of motion pictures. She received an Academy Award for her brilliant performance as Mildred Pierce *in 1945. In addition to her theatrical interests, she was elected to the Board of Directors of the PepsiCola Corporation. Her death ended 45 years of screen stardom.*

Time

How many times a day have you heard a person say, "I never have enough time"?

Or if one is lucky, "the time was right."

If unlucky, "well, the time was wrong."

Time is one aspect of life that we all share, to make of it what we will. It is up to us to make time to love, time to give, time to pray. Time to think gives us purity of thought, the courage to carry on and the dignity to stand tall through the good and the bad.

After all, it is our time, God-given in His wisdom, and if we ask His guidance on how to use it, time becomes one of the most precious gifts we have.

MY WORD!

Robert Bloch

Known best for his chilling novel that was the basis of the Alfred Hitchcock film, Psycho, *Robert Bloch is the prolific writer of dozens of mystery, suspense and science fiction novels and hundreds of short stories.*

Cooperation

Every writer's life is a love story, a romance between man and lexicon. As an author, I've always been infatuated with words, and there are some which I have special reasons for cherishing. Psycho, for example, is one I'm not likely to forget.

In recent years, however, I'm less concerned with words per se and more concerned with meanings. And, of all the words I know, one seems most relevant today.

We live in a competitive society, a society of stress and strife, a society filled with failures, follies and frustrations which are the direct result of the continuing need to compete.

But what if competition could be replaced by **cooperation**?

Cooperation. A clumsy-looking word, not very euphonious, scarcely eloquent or elegant, but how important!

For cooperation is the cornerstone of all human relationships between parent and child, husband and wife, employer and employee, citizen and state, between friends, relatives, coworkers, people in every walk of life and every circumstance.

Saints and sages have always urged that we love one another, but for many of us, this seems an impossible ideal; our emotional resources cannot be extended to that degree.

Lesser than love, yet far more practicable, is cooperation. Doing unto others, doing with others, doing for others. That's the meaning of the word I'd select, a word which can be the key to our survival and our salvation.

Fran Capo

Dubbed Fast Talker Extraordinaire by the Associated Press, Miss Capo is listed in the Guinness Book of World Records *as being clocked speaking at a rate of 603.32 words per minute. Born in Greenwich Village and raised in Queens, New York, Fran has performed her comedy in clubs throughout the United States. Because of her many talents, she's been seen on network TV including "Entertainment Tonight," "Good Morning America," "CNN's Larry King Live," and "The Late Show."*

Her career includes being a stand-up comedienne, writer, humorous lecturer and doing voice-overs for cartoons. She started her multifaceted career as part of the WBLS-FM radio morning crew in New York City. Each morning, listeners could hear the sultry weather and traffic reports of June East, long-lost sister of Mae West, and Fran's alter ego.

Her audio cassette tape of Fran's Fast Fractured Fairy Tales *has become a collector's item as she presents a series of classic tales from* The Three Little Pigs *to* Rumplestiltskin. *All are told intelligibly at the speed of sound, intertwining her character voices, fast talking and comedic ability to give the stories a clever and humorous twist.*

Creativity

As a stand-up comic I have a lot of favorite words. As a fast talker I try to use them all in ten seconds. But the word I have decided on as my favorite is the word **creativity**.

Creativity allows one to take what people consider impossible and make it happen. Creativity expands the mind and gives you a fresh and different perspective on the same subject. Creativity is a spark that begins inside you and grows with passion until it is something the world can see.

Creativity has brought us spectacular movies, new inventions, wonderful books, unique art. Creativity is limitless. It gave birth to my son as the world's youngest comic, allowed me to meet a wonderful man in a new way, and gave me a career of freedom, adventure and travel.

Creativity . . . the possibilities are endless.

Nancy Kassebaum

Nancy Kassebaum

Nancy Landon Kassebaum was introduced to the world of politics at an early age. The daughter of Alfred M. Landon, who was the 1936 Republican presidential nominee and Governor of Kansas, Kassebaum grew up listening to political discussions between her father and the many journalists and political figures who came to visit him. Her family background provided her with a unique environment that spurred her intense interest in the world of politics.

Serving three terms in the United States Senate, she become the Chairman of the Labor and Human Resources Committee, the first woman ever to head a Senate committee. She is known as a coalition builder in the Senate and has earned the respect of her peers as an independent thinker.

Senator Kassebaum raised her four children on a farm in Maize, Kansas, where she served on the school board. She holds a Master's Degree in diplomatic history from the University of Michigan as well as a Bachelor's Degree in political science from the University of Kansas.

MY WORD!

Grammy

Can anything give more immediate and lasting pleasure than catching a glimpse of the world through a child's eyes? Shelley captured all this wonderment perfectly when he observed that a child has "... a spirit yet streaming from the waters of baptism; it is to believe in love, to believe in loveliness, to believe in belief; it is to be so little that the elves can reach to whisper in your ear; it is to turn pumpkins into coaches, and mice into horses, and lowness into loftiness, and nothing into everything, for each child has its fairy godmother in its soul."

When I was first elected to the Senate, I said that Mother was still my most important title. Then I became a grandmother and discovered I had gotten a promotion. Today I can answer the phone, hear a little voice pipe "Grammy!" and know that once again the elves will whisper in my ear, too.

So **Grammy** is my favorite word, but Mother will always be a close second . . . a very close second.

L. Ron Hubbard

In a lifetime of creation and productivity, L. Ron Hubbard achieved global stature as a writer and educator, mariner and explorer, philosopher and humanitarian. As a writer, known to millions of readers throughout the world, he has been acclaimed as one of the most prolific, widely read and influential authors of the twentieth century.

Born in Tilden, Nebraska, and raised in the rugged outdoors of Montana, he was a world traveler before he was 19, studied at George Washington University and Princeton, and became a member of the Explorer's Club who headed up many expeditions of discovery. Hubbard's literary career spanned more than half a century and encompassed more than 550 published works. His fiction ranged in genres from adventure, western, mystery and suspense to science fiction. His non-fiction writings cover diverse subject areas of societal and cultural significance, from self-help and the ethical and spiritual nature of man to art and music, drug rehabilitation, education and management.

Nearly 120 million copies of L. Ron Hubbard's works have been sold in 30 languages and 115 countries. His name and books continue to appear on best-seller lists and to garner awards and accolades around the world.

Freedom

My word is **freedom**, one which in Greece, Rome, England, Colonial America, France and Washington has been the subject of much conversation.

The main trouble with freedom is that it does not have an anatomy. Something that is free is free. It is not free with wires, vias, by-passes or dams; it is simply free.

Minus-freedom is entrapment; and if one wants to understand existence and his unhappiness with it, he must understand entrapment and its mechanisms.

In what can a person become entrapped? Basically and foremost, he can become entrapped in ideas. In view of the fact that freedom and ability can be seen to be somewhat synonymous, ideas of disability are above all an entrapment.

There is the story of fishing in Lake Tanganyika where the sun's rays, being equatorial, pierce burningly to the lake's bottom. The natives there fish by tying a number of slats of wood on a long piece of line. They take either end of this line and put it in canoes, and then paddle the two canoes to shore, the slatted line stretching between. The sun shining downward presses the shadows of these bars down to the bottom of the lake and thus a cage of shadows moves inward toward the shallows. The fish, seeing this cage contract upon them, which is composed of nothing but

L. Ron Hubbard (continued)

the absence of light, flounder frantically into the shallows where they cannot swim, and are thus caught, picked up in baskets and cooked. There is nothing to be afraid of but shadows.

In the past, a knowledge of his own character was often an unpalatable fact to man, since people sought to force him to achieve knowledge of himself solely through condemnation. He resisted what he was, and he became what he resisted. Ever in a dwindling spiral, he reached lower dregs. If ever once a man were to realize with accuracy what he was, if he were to realize what other people sought to make him, and if he could attain this knowledge with great certainty, there would be no chains strong enough to prevent his escaping; for such would be his astonishment that he would brave beasts, gods and Lucifer himself to become something better than what he had beheld in his own heart.

Acknowledgment is made to L. Ron Hubbard Library for permission to reproduce a selection from the copyrighted works of L. Ron Hubbard.

Cesar Romero

Cesar Romero was born in New York City of Cuban parentage. The talented actor was known as the "Latin lover" of numerous films as well as in sophisticated character parts. Some of his memorable roles included Doc Holiday in Frontier Marshal, *the title role in* The Cisco Kid, *as Cortez in* Captain from Castile, *and as The Joker in the popular "Batman" television series. He was known for the interest he took in numerous charitable causes, and his word is an appropriate one in view of his many personal commitments.*

Responsibility

Responsibility is something that we are all born to face. Consciously or unconsciously, it is always there.

Man and woman have a responsibility to each other as husband and wife. They in turn have a responsibility to their children. If in public life, one has a responsibility to the people, to the public that one serves. All in turn have a responsibility to their country, their community, to their family and to their God.

Life itself is a responsibility and, like it or not, it must be faced with courage and integrity.

Barry Goldwater

Barry Morris Goldwater served in the United States Senate representing the state of Arizona from 1953 to 1987 as a conservative Republican. He is a native of Phoenix and was active in the United States Air Force as a pilot during World War II. In the Senate, he was chairman of the Armed Services Committee and ran for the presidency in 1964 on the Republican ticket. His honors include recognition from many organizations, and he is the author of several books including The Conscience of a Conservative, Where I Stand, The Face of Arizona *and* People and Places. *An active and enthusiastic sportsman, he was among the first non-Native Americans to navigate the Grand Canyon's Colorado River.*

Love

I have a feeling that the word I will submit to you has been submitted by many, many others. I pick the word **love**, not for any particular one of many connotations or meanings, but just the word as it is generally applied to living with people in this world. If we had more love and less hate, maybe we would start making progress toward the peaceful world we all envision.

Morris Fishbein, M.D.

A physician and editor for a number of years of The Journal of the American Medical Association *and* Medical World News, *Dr. Morris Fishbein wrote numerous syndicated newspaper columns while having an enormous influence on medical politics. This native of St. Louis maintained a medical practice in Chicago until 1913, when he became assistant editor of JAMA. He was named editor in 1924 and was generally considered to be the voice of the AMA until his retirement in 1949. He also served as editor of* Hygeia, the Bulletin of the Society of Medical History, *and was a contributing editor for twenty years for* Postgrad Medicine *and for eight years for* McCall's. *He died in 1976 at 87 years of age.*

Uncertain

Since medicine is not an absolute science, some favorite words of science writers are "possibly" and "probably." A commission appointed by the Food and Drug Administration to indicate drugs that are effective made four classifications: "effective," "possibly effective," "probably effective," and "not effective."

Many a medical writer attempting conclusions on the results of his studies is likely to say: "These results seem to show . . ." or "These results indicate . . ."

The only thing certain in life is death. With the new techniques for restoring respiration and heartbeat, the doctor can only say the patient "seems to be dead."

Giles T. Brown

Photo by Jarett Snider

Retired Dean of the California State University at Fullerton, California, Dr. Brown has continued his career as a world traveler and lecturer on the people and lands he has encountered. He has utilized his perspective on world affairs from personal observations and interviews with international leaders to provide his audiences with a unique insight into global events. He is an active volunteer in the Friends of the Library on the University of California's Irvine campus.

MY WORD!

Window

Words are windows to the world, and the word **window** is one of my favorite words.

Recently while in Asia, I joined a group which chartered an airplane flying into a remote valley in the highlands of western New Guinea. After landing, we visited a tribe of humans who were still using stone axes. They had no horses, burros, oxen or animals larger than the pig to help them with their work. Their language was completely verbal except for the attempts of a missionary to put some of their words into writing. They had no word for zebra, elephant, automobile, television or chess since none of these existed in the valley. To them, even the word window was unknown.

Because of its long development, the English language has many words which serve as windows to enrich life. People who have spoken it have had a variety of experiences in travel, business, government and the arts. Actually, the English language itself is a composite window as large as life, as limitless as space and as human as any of us. These are reasons I enjoy words and why the word window is a favorite.

Giles T. Brown (continued)

A window is an outreach to the unknown, the different, the exciting, the useful and the beautiful. Physical windows are with us through life. It is through them we see the world from our home while a child, from our school while young, from our factories and offices while working, and from our cars or jets while traveling. Yet these views are limited by our eyesight, and when evening comes the view shrinks to those few areas which can be seen despite the darkness.

But words as windows are not limited by time or distance. They free us from the routine, the banal and the mediocre. They stimulate and inspire us to see other places, do other things and think other thoughts. They enrich our lives and let us live.

Eugene McCarthy

Presidential aspirant and former Democratic Senator from Minnesota, Eugene McCarthy was noted for his liberal thinking and opposition to the unpopular war in Vietnam. He campaigned heavily for the nomination of his party in 1968 against Lyndon Johnson and Robert Kennedy. Ultimately, Hubert H. Humphrey was chosen at the Chicago convention in an attempt to reunite the party.

McCarthy then became an independent candidate for President at the 1968 and other national elections.

Silence

Replying to a request for my favorite word is very difficult. There are so many good words, some of them are well used, some badly used, and some used rarely if at all. Some words are best in context; some are good either in or out of context. I have concluded that my favorite word is **silence**, since in oral communication it opens the field to all words.

Bob Mathias

Bob Mathias, a native of Tulare, California, gained worldwide attention by winning the Olympic Decathlon Gold Medal in London at the age of seventeen, and repeated this amazing feat in Helsinki, setting Olympic and world records. After graduating from Stanford, he served in the United States Marines and later starred in four major motion pictures. He also was a sports commentator for televised athletic events. He was elected to the United States House of Representatives in 1966, and served in three Congresses on the Agriculture and Foreign Affairs Committees.

His numerous awards include being named recipient of the Sullivan Award as the outstanding amateur athlete of the year and the Theodore Roosevelt Award, the most prestigious recognition given an individual from the NCAA He served as director of the Olympic Training Center at Colorado Springs and as executive director of the National Fitness Foundation. Today, Bob is active in public relations activities and is in demand as a motivational speaker.

MY WORD!

Stick-to-itiveness

When competing on the athletic field, I found that one of the first decisions you must make if you're going to excel is that you possess **stick-to-itiveness**, the will and the determination to stick with it. Very early in my athletic career, I spotted a quotation that sums this up, "A winner never quits, and a quitter never wins."

I have kept this in mind always, for it applies in every aspect of life, whether you're pushing an exhausted body on to complete ten events in the decathlon, or trying to get a bill through Congress.

I've had the opportunity to speak to many young people throughout this country and the world, and the one thing I always tell them is that setting goals is pointless unless you also make up your mind to have the stick-to-itiveness to reach those goals.

Art Linkletter is perhaps the best-known native of Moose Jaw, Saskatchewan. This popular radio and television personality earned fame as the host of a long-running feature known as "The House Party." The show ran every weekday afternoon for a quarter of a century.

Linkletter's twenty books have included Kids Say the Darndest Things, a compilation of some of the humorous comments he has collected over the years, Confessions of a Happy Man, Drugs at My Doorstep and I Didn't Do It Alone. His "People Are Funny" show resulted in additional fame and fortune, but he has always continued to recall the days when he was a struggling young announcer coping with the daily trials and tribulations of the world of entertainment. As one who was one of the innovators of radio and TV's stunt shows, he has brought laughter and enjoyment to hundreds of millions of listeners and viewers over the years.

Crisis

I have chosen **crisis** as my special word. It has been a constant companion of mine for more than fifty years in the exciting business of broadcasting. Radio and television, by their nature, produce a steady stream of crises; the pilot, or audition, must face the critical eye of the network, the sponsor, and the star. The tension of meeting a deadline to produce creative material, timed to the second, and ready to go when the red light flashes. The acid test of audience response, week after week, having to compete with other shows on other channels at the same time. For many, a broadcasting career is a quick road to ulcers and nervous disorders.

But to the person who seizes each crisis as an opportunity to excel at the supreme moment of testing, the word takes on the meaning best illustrated by the character in Chinese picture writing. In the Orient the word "crisis" is represented by two drawings. One is for "danger" and the other is for "opportunity."

Michael Strumpf

English Professor Michael Strumpf is said to be the most popular instructor on the Moorpark Community College campus in California. A native of New York City, he has hosted The National Grammar Hotline since 1971. Three hundred or more people call his office each week with questions regarding punctuation, proper forms of address and sentence structure. His calls are from other teachers, students, government officials, writers and TV producers. He's even heard from the Secretary to the President of the United States with a question regarding proper usage. He can be called from 8:00 a.m. to 12:30 p.m. weekdays (PST) at (805) 378-1494 for scholarly advice of a grammatical nature.

His appearances on "Today," the "Charles Osgood File" and the "CBS Evening News" and numerous radio shows have acclaimed him as The Grammar Guru.

Some of his publications include Painless Perfect Grammar, Websters New World Abbreviations and Acronyms, Fundamentals of Grammar and Writing *and* The Grammar Bible.

Scholarly

Choosing a favorite word certainly was a brainteaser. As a professor of English, I deal with words. As the author of "The Grammar Bible" and recipient of hundreds of calls weekly on The National Grammar Hot Line, I am awash with words. My heavens, what a task to choose just one.

However, I do have a word. It is **scholarly**. I meet with so many people. Some of them are students: clock watchers, dreamers, non-scholars. But, a scholarly individual is one who is unceasingly seeking after the truth, is honestly endeavoring to find answers, and will go to any lengths to find those answers. Scholasticism implies honesty, integrity, hard work, time and ethics. A scholarly person is one to be sought after, for he/she will probably often be in trouble. Students avoid pitfalls, roadblocks. Scholars look assiduously for them, confront their challenge, and try with all their powers to overcome.

I am not always scholarly, but I hold the word as as shining light to illuminate the dark paths to the vessel of knowledge.

Johnny Mercer

Johnny Mercer was a native of Savannah, Georgia. This master composer and lyricist was honored by election to the Songwriters Hall of Fame for his more than fifteen hundred songs featured on the "Hit Parade," in films and on the Broadway stage. His lengthy and productive career included his collaboration with many of the time's top tunesmiths. Some of his more memorable melodies and lyrics include "That Old Black Magic," "Accent-to-ate the Positive," "Blues in the Night," "Moon River," "Days of Wine and Roses," "Laura" and "Jeepers Creepers."

Prior to his musical success, he was a stage actor and vocalist with several bands. His inability to read music proved to be no handicap to his career. He was the recipient of four Oscars from the Academy of Motion Picture Arts and Sciences for songs he wrote for the silver screen. He was an active member of the prestigious American Society of Composers, Authors and Publishers and one of the founders of Capitol Records.

He lived in Palm Springs, California, until the time of his death in 1976.

MY WORD!

Butterfly

My favorite word is **butterfly**.

A Frenchman, Spaniard, Englishman and German were discussing which was the most beautiful language, and the Englishman said, "Of course, there is no question that English is. Take the word butterfly, for example. Where would you find a prettier sound, and picture, that says exactly what it sounds like? By all means, English!"

To which the Frenchman almost sighed, "But, monsieur, papillion! Papillion is softer, prettier and says infinitely more! By all means, French!"

And the Spaniard almost condescendingly said "Ah, gentlemen, indeed two mellifluous words, and very beautiful but tell me truly, do you think either can compare with mariposa? It says it all, and enchantingly!"

The German drew himself to a straight attention and, clicking his heels, said fiercely and gutturally, "Ja, gentlemen, but what is wrong with schmetterlinck?"

Hank Ketcham

"I'M GONNA HANG YA UP NOW, MARGARET. MY EARS ARE ALL FULL OF *WORDS!*"

Henry King Ketcham is Seattle born and lived in Switzerland for many years prior to his return to California in 1977. After early work with Walter Lantz at Universal Studios and Walt Disney Productions, he created Dennis the Menace in 1950. This led to success in several areas of the media as this young protagonist captured the imagination and love of millions, in spite of his "limited vocabulary."

MY WORD!

There must be a word . . .

Dennis has been "going on six" for more than forty-five years and has a normal vocabulary of more than three thousand words, many of them pronounced in a rather arbitrary fashion but nonetheless understood. His enunciability is somewhat limited, so certain modifications invariably appear in his speech, and in my captions.

Such as: "Ya wanna know somethin'?" and "Well, what are ya gonna do 'bout it?" Or he will use big words like "kiddigarter" and "telebishion."

As he regularly becomes five the day following his sixth birthday, I see little opportunity for improvement. I'm trapped in a three thousand word rut. I don't know why . . . but, in spite of this handicap, Dennis continues to come through loud and clear.

There must be a word for it.

Index by Name

Allen, George viii
Ambrose, Stephen 64
Anders, William 100
Armour, Dr. Richard viii
Asimov, Isaac viii
Ash, Mary Kay 33
Baldridge, Letitia 48
Ball, Lucille 92
Barry, Dave 54
Bloch, Robert 123
Bombeck, Erma 12
Boone, Pat 94
Boyd, Malcolm 58
Brennan, Walter 118
Brothers, Dr. Joyce 110
Brown, Dr. Giles 134
Buscaglia, Dr. Leo 8
Campbell, Glen 104
Caniff, Milton 80
Capo, Fran 124
Claus, Santa 78
Cox, Danny 30
Crawford, Joan 122
Crichton, Michael 50
De Toledano, Ralph 74
Dean, Jimmy 44
Deford, Frank 20
DeVos, Dick 4
Dial, Joan 88
Eagle, Herbert 27
Embery, Joan 99
Espy, Willard 7
Fishbein, Dr. Morris 133
Forbes, Timothy 70

Ford, President Gerald 114
Gallup, George 86
Getty, J. Paul ix
Ginzberg, Ralph viii
Golden, Harry 87
Goldwater, Barry 132
Graham, Rev. Billy 96
Harmon, Tom 62
Harris, T George viii
Hesburgh, Father Theodore 42
Hills, Lee 73
Hilton, Conrad x
Hubbard, L. Ron 128
Jansen, Dan 121
Jonak, Chuck 60
Karcher, Carl 24
Kassebaum, Nancy 126
Kemp, Jack 52
Kent, Corita ix
Ketcham, Hank 146
King, Stephen 26
Knebel, Fletcher 66
Knott, Walter 82
Landers, Ann 90
Landry, Tom 38
Levin, Ira ix
Linkletter, Art 140
Lord, Walter ix
Mathias, Bob 138
McCarthy, Eugene 137
McDonald, Ronald 6
McGrory, Mary ix
Meglin, Nick 18
Mercer, Johnny 144
Milsap, Ronnie 10
Mondavi, Robert 46
Nixon, Patricia 22
Pei, Mario 91
Popenoe, Dr. Paul 39

Reagan, President Ronald	2
Renault, Mary	57
Risner, General Robinson	36
Romero, Cesar	131
Sanders, Colonel Harland	108
Schuller, Dr. Robert	16
Scott, Willard	1
Scully, Vin	84
Sharman, Bill	ix
Siegel, Dr. Bernie	28
Speakes, Larry	116
Starr, Bart	76
Staubach, Roger	72
Strumpf, Michael	142
Teller, Edward	x
Thomas, Lowell	113
Van Buren, Abigail	14
Vanderbilt, Amy	viii
Viscott, Dr. David	68
Welk, Lawrence	34
White, Kate	56
Whitman, Christine Todd	106
Willson, Meredith	43
Wolper, David	101
Wouk, Herman	102
Wrigley, Phillip K.	viii
Zumwalt, Admiral Elmo	40

Index by Word

Adventure	30
Affirmative	114
American	70
Animals	99
Appreciate	104
Attitude	76
Beauty	92
Behemoth	7
Butterfly	144
Caring	22
Challenge	10
Civility	42
Clearly	106
Communications	40
Cooperation	123
Creativity	124
Crisis	140
Daddy	94
Decision	96
Dictionary	73
Duty	64
Effort	121
Enthusiasm	113
Excel	46
Explore	100
Faith	36
Family	24, 116
Forgiveness	86
Freedom	128
Giving	78
God	1
Grammy	126
Harmony	88
Home	2, 84
Hope	4

Humility	62
Idea	52
Integrity	108
Laughter	6
Love	8, 28, 39, 132
Meanwhile	80
Mesmerize	48
Mesopotamia	68
No	14, 102
Now	20
Perseverence	72, 82
Persistent	38
Planning	101
Possible	16
Responsibility	131
Righteous	60
Rosemary	43
Scholarly	142
Sell	27
Separate	118
Silence	137
Stick-to-itiveness	18, 138
Symbol	50
Tenacity	44
Tenderness	110
Tenebrous	26
Thing	87
Thridge	66
Time	122
Try	90
We	58
Weasel	54
Window	134
Wonderful	34
Wow	56
Words	146
Yes	12
You can	33

About the author

Vick Knight, Ed.D. says his love of words began as a student at Hollywood High School, was nurtured through his undergraduate years at the University of Southern California and bloomed into a passion during his career as a teacher and school administrator. Now, as Dean of the School of Education at Newport University, he provides inspirational and motivational programs for audiences throughout the nation, revealing the power of dynamic use of one's vocabulary.

He is the author of numerous books and articles, the host of a series of regional TV programs and writes a column for a daily newspaper. He lives in Southern California with his wife, Carolyn, and enjoys spending leisure time with his four children and six grandchildren.

Order Form

Additional copies of "MY WORD!" may be ordered by using this form.

Please send me _____ copies of "MY WORD!"
@ $9.95 each.   _____

California residents add 7.75 percent tax.   _____

Handling and mailing, $3.00 per book   _____

TOTAL   _____

MAIL ORDERS TO:

Name_____

Address_____

City, State, Zip_____

Send check or mail order, made payable to
Aristan Press
31566 Railroad Canyon Road # 612
Canyon Lake, CA 92587